"This has been Norm and Becky's passion for the twenty-plus years I have known them. It's practical, it's convicting, it's easy. This book is a must-read for all who have been silent too long."

—WILLIAM B. FAY, evangelist, author of *Share Jesus Without Fear*

"You don't have to have the gift of evangelism or an aggressive personality to influence people for Christ when you follow the plans laid out in this book. These nonoffensive methods for reaching neighborhoods can be used by anyone and everyone, regardless of their gifts. Norm and Becky show us what true Team Ministry is."

—LARRY GILBERT, president, Church Growth Institute; author of *Team Ministry* and *Team Evangelism*

"God is exciting and He's ready to transform your neighborhood. Norm and Becky Wretlind's timely and practical book, *When God Is the Life of the Party,* is filled with helpful insights and ideas to get you started and to keep going."

—DR. DICK EASTMAN, international president, Every Home for Christ

"For years Norm and Becky Wretlind have been the pace setters—advocates of relational evangelism. This book is the culmination of a lifetime of experience. I recommend it with great enthusiasm and expectation."

—JOE ALDRICH, Th.D., president emeritus, Multnomah Bible College; author of *Lifestyle Evangelism, Gentle Persuasion, Reunitis* (Prayer Summits)

"'Love your neighbor as yourself' isn't a suggestion. It's a commandment. And there's no better place to start than with *When God Is the Life of the Party.* Norm and Becky Wretlind have written a book that proves anyone can minister to their neighbors in effective, exciting ways. Think you're the only one who is afraid, insecure, or too busy for evangelism? Read this! The Wretlinds have stories from more than twenty years of sharing the good news. And they have ideas for fun, simple ways to impact your neighborhood for Christ. I enthusiastically recommend this book to every believer!"

—LUIS PALAU, evangelist and author

"During their entire adult lives, Norm and Becky Wretlind have led people to Christ by their words and by their lives. In this book they describe one of the most fruitful methods they have used, a method by which they have brought many neighbors to Christ. Read this practical book—it will help make you more effective in bringing your neighbors to the Savior!"

—BILL CONARD, vice president of International Ministries,
Billy Graham Evangelistic Association

"Norm and Becky provide insights into the cultural shifts that have taken place in our communities and then offer practical ways to address them. The book shows how to love not only your neighbor but your whole neighborhood for Jesus' sake. It is a must-read for anyone who wants to get to know their neighbors and then get their neighbors to know Jesus."

—DR. JEFFREY A. JOHNSON, director of evangelism, National Ministries,
American Baptist Churches USA

"Many of us have been waiting for this significant book to be written. Norm and Becky Wretlind personify the message of these pages. They believe that every Christian living in virtually any kind of neighborhood can be used of God to host a party. This book will encourage and help us all to love our neighbors more effectively."

—PAUL CEDAR, D.Min., D.D., chairman, Mission America Coalition

"Norm and Becky Wretlind are no armchair theorists when it comes to sharing the gospel. They are effective practitioners, and in this wonderful book, they show us how we too, through the creative use of hospitality, can reach our friends and neighbors with the hope and love of Christ. What an important and valuable resource!"

—DR. CRAWFORD W. LORITTS JR., speaker; author; radio host;
associate director, Campus Crusade for Christ USA

"Finally a book that not only inspires, but practically equips us to better follow Christ's command to 'love our neighbor'!"

—DWIGHT ROBERTSON, president, Kingdom Building Ministries

WHEN GOD IS THE LIFE OF THE PARTY

Reaching Neighbors Through Creative Hospitality

NORM & BECKY WRETLIND
with JIM KILLAM

NAVPRESS®

BRINGING TRUTH TO LIFE

OUR GUARANTEE TO YOU

We believe so strongly in the message of our books that we are making this quality guarantee to you. If for any reason you are disappointed with the content of this book, return the title page to us with your name and address and we will refund to you the list price of the book. To help us serve you better, please briefly describe why you were disappointed. Mail your refund request to: NavPress, P.O. Box 35002, Colorado Springs, CO 80935.

NAVPRESS
P.O. Box 35001
Colorado Springs, CO 80935

The Navigators is an international Christian organization. Our mission is to reach, disciple, and equip people to know Christ and to make Him known through successive generations. We envision multitudes of diverse people in the United States and every other nation who have a passionate love for Christ, live a lifestyle of sharing Christ's love, and multiply spiritual laborers among those without Christ.

NavPress is the publishing ministry of The Navigators. NavPress publications help believers learn biblical truth and apply what they learn to their lives and ministries. Our mission is to stimulate spiritual formation among our readers.

ISBN 1-57683-437-9

Cover design by Ray Moore
Cover photos by Ryan McVay/Getty Images; Yellow Dog Productions/Getty Images; Masterfile
Creative Team: Kent Wilson, Keith Wall, Kathy Mosier, Glynese Northam

Most of the anecdotal illustrations in this book are true to life and are included with the permission of the persons involved. Where indicated, other illustrations are composites of real situations, and any resemblance to people living or dead is coincidental.

Unless otherwise identified, all Scripture quotations in this publication are taken from the HOLY BIBLE: NEW INTERNA-TIONAL VERSION® (NIV®). Copyright © 1973, 1978, 1984 by International Bible Society. Used by permission of Zondervan Publishing House. All rights reserved. Other versions used include: THE MESSAGE (MSG). Copyright © 1993, 1994, 1995, 1996, 2000, 2001, 2002. Used by permission of NavPress Publishing Group; the Holy Bible, New Living Translation, (NLT) copyright © 1996. Used by permission of Tyndale House Publishers, Inc., Wheaton, Illinois 60189. All rights reserved; the New American Standard Bible (NASB), © The Lockman Foundation 1960, 1962, 1963, 1968, 1971, 1972, 1973, 1975, 1977; and the New King James Version (NKJV). Copyright © 1982 by Thomas Nelson, Inc. Used by permission. All rights reserved.

Wretlind, Norm, 1943-
  When God is the life of the party : reaching neighbors through creative hospitality / Norm and Becky Wretlind with Jim Killam.
     p. cm.
Includes bibliographical references.
  ISBN 1-57683-437-9
  1. Evangelistic work. 2. Parties--Religious aspects--Christianity. 3. Neighborliness--Religious aspects--Christianity. I. Wretlind, Becky, 1942- II. Killam, Jim, 1963- III. Title.
  BV3793.W74 2003
  241'.671--dc21
                                        2003013229
Printed in the United States of America
1 2 3 4 5 6 7 8 9 10 / 07 06 05 04 03

FOR A FREE CATALOG OF
NAVPRESS BOOKS & BIBLE STUDIES,
CALL 1-800-366-7788 (USA)
OR 1-416-499-4615 (CANADA)

Dedicated to the Lord of the harvest

and all of our colaborers in that harvest.

Especially, we dedicate this book to our lifelong mentors and models,

Bill and Vonette Bright.

Contents

STAND IN THE CONNECTION GAP

By Bill and Vonette Bright

Despite the amazing scientific and technological advances during the past half-century, something significant has vanished from our modern era. Amid the astounding gains has come a tragic loss — the disappearance of community, connectedness, and cohesiveness that bind people together in meaningful relationships.

Few would disagree that the unraveling of our social fabric, once tightly-woven, has left many towns and neighborhoods threadbare and frayed. Everywhere we go, people tell us they yearn for a sense of belonging, kinship, and close affiliation with others. Yet these God-given needs go largely unmet in our insulated and isolated society.

In her incisive exposé *The Connection Gap: Why Americans Feel So Alone*, journalist Laura Pappano says:

> People talk a great deal about "community" but complain
> of feeling less and less a part of one. People long for rich
> relationships but find themselves wary of committing to
> others. Many of us hunger for intimacy but end up paying

professionals to listen to, care for, and befriend us. . . .

As a society, we face a collective loneliness, an empty feeling that comes not from lack of all human interaction, but from the loss of meaningful interaction, the failure to be a part of something real, or to have faith in institutions that might bring us together. This is what I call the Connection Gap.[1]

As we acknowledge this devastating deficiency, let us also recognize the enormous opportunity it presents for those who seek to share the good news of Jesus Christ. The loosening of relational bonds has created a void we can fill as we love and care for those around us. Indeed, the book in your hands calls all Christians to stand in the connection gap.

There's no doubt that God's plan for mankind included a regular association with other people. That's why His Word contains dozens of instructions about how we're to treat our neighbors. Jesus distilled all this teaching when He was asked to pinpoint the most important commandment. He answered, "'Love the Lord your God with all your heart and with all your soul and with all your mind and with all your strength.' The second is this: 'Love your neighbor as yourself'" (Mark 12:30-31).

The apostle Paul echoed this theme when he said, "The commandments, 'Do not commit adultery,' 'Do not murder,' 'Do not steal,' 'Do not covet,' and whatever other commandment there may be, are summed up in this one rule: 'Love your neighbor as yourself'" (Romans 13:9).

With these challenging thoughts in mind, we believe this book arrives at a critical time. We first met Norm and Becky Wretlind in 1972, and since then we have appreciated their creative approach to evangelism. In fact, the ideas and information presented here are culled from their decades of effective and innovative neighborhood outreach.

In the pages that follow, you will be inspired as you read how God works powerfully through believers who reach out to neighbors. And through an abundance of practical suggestions, you'll learn that sharing the gospel can be natural and nonthreatening. God's Word makes it clear that we are to love our neighbors, and the Wretlinds' book demonstrates the deep joy that comes from fulfilling that commandment.

ACKNOWLEDGMENTS

Under [Christ's] direction, the whole body is fitted together perfectly. As each part does its own special work, it helps the other parts grow, so that the whole body is healthy and growing and full of love.

EPHESIANS 4:16, NLT

Norm and Becky Wretlind:

We have been helped to grow throughout our lives by faithful members of the body of Christ, too numerous to mention. The following are but a few who come to mind:

Mentors who have equipped us: Pastors Harold T. Reese and W. O. Garberson; "Uncle" Johnnie Johnson of Camp Barakel, Michigan; Sara Caballero; Grandma Hull; Ruth Ann Dietz Martin; Rev. Barney Kinard; Dr. Gene A. Getz; George Verwer; Peter Hocking; Bill and Ruth Conard; Brian and Ruth Catalano; Bob George; Dr. Stanley Toussaint; Dr. Jody and Linda Dillow; Dr. Harwood and Pat Hess; Patrick and Barbara McGee; Youth for Christ; Moody Bible Institute; and Campus Crusade for Christ.

Friends who have sustained us: Our many deeply-loved friends in Texas including those at Richland Bible Fellowship Church, especially Dr. Bill and Carol Brewer; those many neighbors and friends quoted in this book; Drs. Frank Minirth and Paul Meier; Doug and Jody Cheney; Floyd and Judy Moreland; Dwight and Hilde Johnson; Don and Joan Criswell; George Simon; Dave and Holly Meehan; our many deeply-loved friends in Colorado, including those at Foothills Bible Church, especially Pastor Bill and Jan Oudemolen, Pastor Brian Boone, Pastor Scott and Lynn Nauman, and Joyce Feil with her Missionary Care Team; Dick and Betty Jo Chadwick; Dr. Al Stirling; Neil and Debbie White; prayer warriors such as Evelyn Peterson, Joan Munroe, Edith Leland, and of course Becky's dad, Ed Horski, and Norm's mom, Lucille Wretlind; our committed Board of Directors for NeighborHope Ministries, including Milt Bryan, Pastor Ken Summers, Steve Fernalld, Jon Bourgain, and Mike Brinks; our office manager, Rick LaFleur; and finally, our secretary, Colleen Pelto.

Family who have cheered us on: Our precious redhead, Miriam, with her doctor-husband, Mike, and their threesome Daniel, Abigail, and Joshua; our sweet Mindi with her pastor-husband, Carey, and their full quiver consisting of Aaron, Melinda, Madeline, Caleb, and Faith; Becky's sister Sharon and her husband, Rusty McKee; and Norm's brother Dr. Dennis O. Wretlind, who helped with the final theological edit.

Finally, we want to publicly thank our coauthor and friend, Jim Killam, for his endless hours and wholehearted effort to produce what you have in your hands. He not only wrote our story but is also putting into practice a lifestyle of loving his neighbors as himself. We are also humbly indebted to Kent Wilson, Executive Publisher of NavPress, for inviting and encouraging us to write this book. Stories of similar passion to reach out to the lost abound in his family history, too. We encourage him to write the next book! ■

Jim Killam:

Thank you, Norm and Becky, for living the Great Commandment like no one else I have ever met. Those who have called you their neighbors are incredibly blessed.

Thank you to my wife, Lauren. Your gifts of helps, mercy, and hospitality helped this book come to life before my eyes. Thanks to our kids, Ben, Zack, and Lindsey, for your patience and understanding during an insanely busy season of interviewing and writing.

And thank you to everyone who prayed faithfully for this project. Without that support, it would not have happened.

Most of all, thank you, God, for using unlikely people in unlikely ways to help build Your kingdom. May this book honor You. ■

THERE'S AN EPIDEMIC IN YOUR NEIGHBORHOOD . . . AND YOU HAVE THE CURE

Imagine that everyone in your neighborhood contracts a disease, one that will prove fatal if they don't get help. Some know they are sick but don't know where to find the right medicine. Others try remedies that seem to ease the pain, but those work only temporarily. Still others don't even know they have the disease and won't know until it's too late.

You, on the other hand, have been given a free, unlimited supply of a miracle drug that will cure the disease. Your own family is well, and you're busy with your own lives. Surely, the neighbors will see how healthy you are and will want to know your secret. If they ask, you'll gladly give them all the medicine they want. You care about them and desire to help them. But you don't want to seem pushy. If they don't approach you, if they just keep to themselves and live with their sickness, it must mean they don't want your help. And they'll die, even though the medicine that would have saved them was right there, just a couple of doors away.

Can you live with that?

For us Christians, that's exactly the situation in our neighborhoods today. And many of us *do* live with it. If our faith is the least bit alive and vibrant, we see the problem clearly. We have what our neighbors need. We want to help them, but we're not even sure how to begin. We feel frustrated that we genuinely desire to assist them but aren't sure how to do so.

The purpose of this book is not to send you on a guilt trip. The fact that you've picked it up in the first place probably means you have the desire and motivation to reach your neighbors with the gospel. We want to equip you with the tools to effectively and naturally reach out to your neighbors with love and kindness. And we want you to know the deep-down joy that results when you and your family touch your neighborhood with the love of Jesus Christ.

We will share with you what we've learned during our more than thirty years of ministering to neighbors and teaching others to do the same: how to meet your neighbors, form friendships, pray for them, care for them, and share Christ with them. We'll offer many ideas for hosting parties and get-togethers in your home, events where neighbors can get to know each other and where the gospel can be shared in a natural and nonthreatening way. Believe us—it can be done.

Throughout these pages, you'll meet people from all walks of life who have amazing stories to tell: stories about lives and neighborhoods that were transformed because Christians took simple steps of obedience to God. There are two common denominators to these stories:

1. The Great Commission is fulfilled when Christians live out the Great Commandment: Love your neighbor as yourself.
2. Successful witnessing happens when Christians take the initiative

to befriend nonChristians, share their experiences of Christ with them, depend on the power of the Holy Spirit, and leave the results to God.

These principles can transform individual lives, marriages, families, and entire neighborhoods. They free us to lovingly engage those who live around us without worrying about how they'll respond. So if you're picking up this book with questions about whether or not God can use you, believe us when we say He can and will. We've been there. You'll read about our early struggles to overcome the fear of reaching out to neighbors. You'll read about how God took our simple acts of obedience to Him and moved in miraculous ways. We'll look at how today's neighborhoods present challenges and obstacles that didn't exist a generation ago. Our current neighborhood in Littleton, Colorado, already had the hidden heartaches common to so many middle-class suburbs when the Columbine High School massacre forever changed us and the way we see our world.

What have we learned over these many years? First, that our mission field happens to be right outside our door, across the street, and down the block. We've also learned that a neighborhood party—an intentional, friendship-building gathering hosted by a Christian—is a powerful approach to demonstrating the love of God to those who don't know Him. In many cases, it's the first time neighbors will ever meet each other, and in some cases, it's the first time they will hear the gospel communicated clearly. Almost always, neighbors begin to feel connected and linked. That sort of feeling lays the groundwork for a neighborhood where people begin caring about each other and opening their homes and their lives to each other.

In the chapters that follow, you'll learn that the powerful ministry of reaching out to your neighborhood requires no special training. We'll focus largely on the impact a husband-and-wife team can have, but any Christian individual can do it. We'll confront the fears that keep Christians from stepping out. We'll talk about specific ways to show hospitality—and, in the process, show Jesus—to your neighbors.

We'll also talk—sometimes from our own painful experiences—about what *not* to do. Your neighbors will sense right away if your outreach is insincere or manipulative. Genuine hospitality requires time, effort, sensitivity, and, most importantly, diligent prayer.

So if you're ready to let God work through you to bless your neighbors, read on. Go ahead and list your reasons why it won't work. We had them, too. Then let this book, through God's leading, address those reasons and your fears. You needn't own a huge house, be a catering whiz, or be the neighborhood social butterfly. All you need is a place you call home—a house, apartment, condo, whatever—and the willingness to let God use you in your neighborhood. The question isn't whether your home is big enough; it's whether your *heart* is big enough.

Here's what we ask of you at the outset: Begin with the belief that God has placed you in your neighborhood for a reason. And regardless of how well you know your neighbors right now, start praying for them. Then don't be surprised when God begins to answer those prayers.

Now, get ready for an adventure that can become the greatest joy of your life.

CHAPTER ONE

THE MAGNET OF HOSPITALITY

Share with God's people who are in need. Practice hospitality.

ROMANS 12:13

Welcome to Anystreet in Yourtown, U.S.A. Join us as we stroll down the sidewalk and take a look around.

There are Bob and Christine, leaving for work. We're not sure of their last name because we've spoken to them only a couple of times. We do know that Bob drives a Saturn, Christine a Toyota. Every morning at 7:30, like clockwork, their garage door slowly rises, just long enough to let Bob's car out. As the car backs toward the street, the garage door closes again, and he's off to work. A few minutes later, Christine's car repeats the same scene.

Then, about 6:00 P.M., it's like watching the same movie backward. The garage door rises, even before we see Bob's Saturn. Finally, the car appears from down the street. Barely even slowing down, the Saturn whips into the driveway and into the garage. The door comes down. Ten minutes later, Christine's car cruises in. Door goes up, door comes down.

That's about all we see of Bob and Christine for days or even weeks at a time. We really don't know much about them other than their taste in cars. They don't have kids. Their house and yard always look neat—almost like those magazine pictures of homes that no one really lives in. Oh, and they have a really powerful garage-door remote that works from at least a block away.

We could talk about how routine comings and goings—loading and unloading the car, carrying groceries in, leaving for work—now often take place behind closed doors and without interaction with neighbors. We could mention how the electric garage-door opener represents the drawbridge to the modern-day castle that so many people make their home. Only when the drawbridge closes is it safe to open the inner door to the house—a house that, on average, is larger than it used to be, though the yard is often smaller.

But we've only been past one house so far. Let's keep walking.

Now we come to the Petersons' house. They moved in a year ago. Nice family. We've talked to Tom and Denise a few times as they were working in the yard. They have three kids, all in elementary school. We *hear* that family more than we see them. They have a big backyard with a six-foot wooden stockade fence. Sometimes we see the kids flailing their arms and legs as they soar above the fence, so we're pretty sure there's a trampoline back there. Tom and Denise built a big deck a couple of months ago. We know because we saw the redwood lumber in the driveway for a week or so. From our upstairs window, we can see that they spend a lot of time out there on summer evenings—not that we're nosy. If they want to keep to themselves, that's their business.

If we didn't have more houses to see, here's where we would talk about how the front porch of yesteryear has been replaced by today's back deck as the home's prime outdoor hangout. We could lament that it's nearly impossible to walk by our neighbors' houses, see them out on their front porches, and stop to shoot the breeze for a few minutes. After all, front yards today are mostly for show. And backyards are surrounded not by a friendly, waist-high picket fence but by one that's tall and imposing. Though we once built fences to keep our kids and pets from running into the street, we now build them with a secondary purpose: to keep out prying eyes and unwanted invaders.

Remember Wilson, the neighbor in the TV sitcom *Home Improvement*? All we ever saw of him were his fishing hat and his eyes, peering over the fence as he dispensed wisdom to Tim the Tool Man. Unfortunately, that was a powerful commentary on backyard America. Even good neighbors, the ones with whom the conversations go beyond small talk, can be mostly obscured by our desire for privacy.

How about that gray house down the street, the one where the drapes are always drawn and the lawn is overgrown? We've never even met those folks. From here, it looks like there's a single mom with a couple of teenagers. The kids always dress in black. One of them had blue hair for a while. Cars come and go over there at all hours of the day and night. The cops have been there a few times. Who knows what's going on behind that front door? We think somebody might be dealing drugs, but that's pretty hard to prove.

This next house belongs to Rick, who went through a divorce two years ago. His ex, Diane, got the kids. We used to talk quite a bit when she was still around, but we've lost that point of contact. Rick's a Christian, but he always seemed hesitant to talk about it. We don't want to push. He's not home much now, and when he is, he usually stays inside. When we think of it, we pray for him. But that isn't all that often. You know what they say: out of sight, out of mind.

This neighborhood hasn't always been so quiet. When there were more families with young kids, we talked a lot more with neighbors. Many of those families have moved out. A few couples besides Rick and Diane got divorced. And the families that haven't moved or split up are so busy with their kids' school and sports activities that they hardly have time to talk. If we're outside, we still wave when they drive by as they speed off to their next event.

Come to think of it, people tend to be a lot more guarded than they were a generation ago. Safety concerns account for part of that. But sometimes it's also because they don't want anyone to know what goes on behind those high fences and closed doors—anything (or everything) from a disorderly house to a crumbling marriage, pornography addiction, child or spousal abuse, or drug dealing. We may not want to believe those problems could be going on just a few paces from our own driveways. But if we're honest with ourselves, we know they do. It doesn't matter whether we live in big cities, suburbs, small towns, or rural areas. People around us are hurting on all kinds of levels.

Not exactly a Norman Rockwell picture so far, is it? For Christians today, just getting to know our neighbors, let alone befriending them and sharing Christ with them, can be a formidable challenge. It's easy just to give up, to tell ourselves that the people behind those fences and castle walls don't want to be bothered. But then, every time we look out our front window, mow the lawn, or walk to the mailbox, we feel that nagging sense of frustration and guilt. Love thy neighbor? We'd settle for *knowing* our neighbors!

Here's one more house. Now this family we like: John and Sue and their kids, Erin and Josh—solid Christians. They invited all the neighbors for an open house when they first moved in last year. John has mentioned that they're going to have a Christmas party this winter, and Sue's talking about starting a neighborhood Bible study. It's not that they're social butterflies—they just seem to intentionally care about people.

Wait a minute. There's somebody home. The front door is open, with just the screen door closed. Let's take a closer look. Get a load of that décor in the living room: knickknacks everywhere, plaques with inspirational sayings, souvenirs from old vacations, scrapbooks, family photos and pictures of other people's families, books all over the place, and a couple of Bibles, too. It's kind of cluttered in there. You'd never see this house pictured in *Better Homes & Gardens*. But still, we like the way this house makes us feel. It's inviting, cozy, and comfortable.

Earlier, a couple of girls from the neighborhood dropped by to ask Sue if she'd show them how to make cookies. And Sue, true to form, set aside what she was doing and invited them in, even though she just got home from her part-time job. Baking cookies may seem like a mundane task, but these girls are obviously delighted. Hospitality seems to be a lost art. Neighbors spending time in the kitchen together? It's such an "Ozzie and Harriet" or "Leave It to Beaver" thing to do. Hardly anyone does that these days.

There's something deeply sad about that. When traditions or activities that once meant something get crowded out or forgotten, it brings a sense of loss. And when that sense of loss combines with factors like stockade fences and garage-door openers, it's no wonder hospitality is so rare and people feel disconnected.

It's not John and Sue's *house* that attracts people. There's nothing remarkable about it. It's the people. The spirit of Christ seems to radiate there, and it isn't just for that family—it's for this neighborhood.

We're sure glad they moved in.

TIMES HAVE CHANGED, PEOPLE HAVE NOT

Maybe the previous scenario is stereotypical. Granted, not every home in every neighborhood looms like a well-protected fortress. In plenty of neighborhoods today, especially those with younger children, casual friendships do develop over time. But most people would agree that true hospitality—extending love and generosity to guests—is rare, even among Christians.

Neighborhoods may have changed, but people today are not all that different from those a generation ago. Maybe they're busier and more stressed. There definitely are more broken homes and more drugs available. But people's need for God and their need for love and friendship aren't any different. It just takes more time and effort on the part of Christians today to build bridges, to fit into somebody's life.

Our first house, purchased in the late 1960s, was located in Anaheim, California. Typical of people in suburban neighborhoods with young families, the neighbors on our cul-de-sac interacted regularly. A comfortable sense of community existed. Divorce was still rare and families were, by and large, stable. People drank alcohol, of course, but drugs still were something those crazy hippies did. Crime was almost nonexistent in our neighborhood. We didn't lock our doors or worry about leaving things in the yard overnight. Neighbors got together for block parties, volleyball, even a neighborhood bowling league. Getting to know people was easy. Neighbors freely invited us into their homes and backyards.

Whatever might have changed, there has always been a difference between simple, neighborly hospitality and *Christian* hospitality, which carries with it the sincere purpose of loving people into God's kingdom. Even in that friendly, comfortable Anaheim neighborhood, for the first three years we lived there we were frustrated by our fear to share our faith with neighbors, which resulted in a bitter fight between the two of us. After fervent prayer, God showed us that it wasn't nearly as difficult as we'd imagined. The sense of hospitality that already existed provided a natural springboard to share Christ, simply by taking the initiative to be open about our faith and our feelings.

We don't have that head start today. In many neighborhoods, it's rare even to see people outside. Unless you make a concerted effort, how are you going to interact with your neighbors? With an implicit "Do Not Disturb" sign hanging on most front doors, how can a Christian family hope to have an impact on the people around them?

It might surprise you to learn that most of those overworked, private people in your neighborhood desperately would like to know you, too. People who don't know their neighbors feel a sense of loneliness and isolation, regardless of how many friendships they have in other places.

Every time we have organized a simple little neighborhood gathering, the majority of the neighbors show up. Consistent with basic human nature, they long to feel connected, wanted, and cared for. People from any walk of life desire to be invited to do something with other individuals or couples.

Christian hospitality today rarely *just happens*. In every neighborhood we've lived in, friendly or otherwise, we have found evangelistic holiday parties to be one of the most effective icebreakers. These parties often have been the first time that some of our neighbors actually met each other. We plan the event carefully, always including a time of sharing based on a seasonal topic. As you'll learn in chapters 6 and 7, these conversations aren't at all awkward, and they don't send people scurrying for the door. Instead, they *open* doors to something beyond small talk.

That's the beginning of a neighborhood transformation. From there, anything can happen, as we later learned when we moved from Anaheim to the Dallas suburb of Richardson, Texas. A true neighborhood fellowship grew there, built around Bible studies in people's homes. And it all was based upon Christian warmth and sincere hospitality. When even one Christian extends that to a neighborhood, it attracts people like a magnet. We'll let one of our former neighbors in Richardson relate those days.

King Nash:

My wife, Dottie, and I were one of the first couples to move into that new neighborhood in the early 1970s. The first neighbors who moved next door to us were Barbara and Patrick McGee. They were such irresistible people. They always had a smile and they exuded peace, which I didn't have. They were superfriendly, always gentle and mild-mannered, always volunteering to help.

We had been in new neighborhoods before, but this one was different. Most of the people who moved in had fairly young children, so we had a lot in common that way. It was the social activities that divided people. You had the partyers and you had the Christians . . . but I guess most everyone considered themselves Christians of some sort.

Although Dottie and I called ourselves Christians, we really were not dedicated. When Barbara and Patrick invited us next door for Bible studies, we went more as a social thing than anything else. It was a way to meet people. The McGees were close friends of Norm and Becky, who moved in a year or two after we did. Those two couples became instrumental in neighborhood Bible studies and parties that were religious in nature.

Initially, I went without resistance but without much enthusiasm either. My enthusiasm grew as I got to know some of the people and became more serious about the Bible study. I was kind of attracted like a moth to a light, I guess, by the outgoing personalities of the McGees and the friendship and kindness they extended to us. It was just pleasant to associate with them. And then when other people got involved, it turned into a nice social arrangement.

As things developed, some of the party-type people started coming to the Bible studies and became seriously converted. A couple of the guys were in sales and were making a lot of money. They previously had not been religious at all. One guy and his wife were always having parties at their house, but he felt depressed and unfulfilled. I remember him saying to me, "I'm the one with the swimming pool. How come I'm not having any fun?"

When some of these partyers got really involved in the study, that was an incentive for some of the other people to investigate it. I can hardly explain the amazing growth that took place in a neighborhood where one normally would have expected a lot of resistance.

I don't think some of them were really seeking a religious experience at first. But when people get together with a group of Christians who are having a good time without being smashed and are comfortable with themselves and with others, there's a good feeling that's created.

No one felt they were being pushed or conned into anything. There was no pressure. That's important. People nowadays don't like high-pressure sales for anything, not even for a good product.

With the help of Patrick McGee, I went over the hump and made a commitment to Christ. I was part of a miraculous growth story that started with two couples and became an entire neighborhood church. I know times have changed, but if those same people went back and started over in any neighborhood anywhere, I think they would transform it. ■

STEPPING OUT IN FAITH

You'll read much more about that neighborhood and about developing a neighborhood fellowship in chapter 8. For now, we would quibble with only one point in King's story: God did indeed use the McGees and us in that suburban Dallas neighborhood, but *He* did the transforming. We simply responded out of obedience and sincerely loved our neighbors. We left the results to God.

We still look back in amazement at those years when more than sixty neighbors came to know Christ in the first three years we lived in that neighborhood. Living there was like being part of the early church: "Every day they continued to meet together in the temple courts. They broke bread in their homes and ate together with glad and sincere hearts, praising God and enjoying the favor of all the people. *And the Lord added to their number daily those who were being saved*" (Acts 2:46-47, emphasis added).

No matter what your neighborhood looks like to you today, whether you've already opened your home and lives or simply would like to take the first step, the most important recommendation we can give you is this: It starts with earnest, believing prayer.

We are active members of the Mission America Coalition, a national initiative of evangelical denominations and ministries dedicated to empowering every Christian to be a beacon to his or her neighborhood. By application, that means covering your neighborhood first through praying, then through active caring, and finally through sharing Christ. Try walking through your neighborhood regularly, praying for the residents of each home as you walk by. Make a list of homes and names. Pray that God will prepare those people, just as He prepares you to reach out to them. Pray for encounters, conversations, friendships, opportunities to show hospitality, and open doors to share Christ. Then be ready for God's answers, and be obedient to His leading.

During the time early in our marriage when we did not have an effective neighborhood ministry, we used to pray regularly for lost souls. But it wasn't until we began to engage in friendships with our nonChristian neighbors that we felt a passion for the lost. At that point, God worked in our hearts as we made our time available and sought opportunities to love our neighbors.

Hospitality today often occurs "by invitation only." Why not be the family in your neighborhood who issues that irresistible invitation?

LOVE THY NEIGHBORHOOD

Each of you should look not only to your own interests, but also to the interests of others.   PHILIPPIANS 2:4

When most couples move into a new neighborhood, they hope for the best: friendly families with well-behaved children who drop by once in a while (always at the perfect time) with a plate of cookies or perhaps with an offer to mow the lawn.

Too often what we get is something short of residential utopia: streets, subdivisions, and cities full of busy people who barely have enough time and energy to tend to their own lives, let alone take an active interest in their neighbors. On a good day, we get eye contact and a quick wave. On a bad day, we get the guy from three houses down stomping across our front yard, cussing at Rex, his unruly beagle. (Hey, at least we know the *dog's* name now.)

And often we feel guilty. Guilty that we don't find the time or muster the courage to knock on a neighbor's door or approach her in the yard to strike up a conversation. Guilty that our neighborhood seems cold and unfriendly and that we're not helping matters. And, most importantly for Christians, guilty that our home is not a lighthouse beaming God's love and grace. These feelings of guilt raise the questions, "How can we establish connections—and eventually real, caring friendships—with the people behind those doors and beyond those fences? How can we be strong Christian witnesses to our neighbors without coming off as too pious and goody-two-shoes to be taken seriously?"

Before you can reach your neighbors with the love of Christ, you need to know and care about them. That's hardly a profound thought, and in generations past we wouldn't even have needed to write this chapter. If you're lucky enough today to live in a neighborhood where people talk and even do things together, much of this chapter may sound overly simplistic. But in an age of bedroom communities, double-income families, closed doors, and high fences, we're not going to assume that you even know all of your neighbors' names or would recognize them at the mall.

Whatever type of neighborhood you live in (urban, suburban, or rural; old or new; blue-collar, white-collar, or mixed), the common relationship is simple: You and your neighbors all reside there and share a stake in making it a good place to live. For some, that stake is only about preserving property value, but it's there nevertheless.

In this book, we'll talk about neighborhoods in their obvious sense— the place where you live. Remember, though, that your true "neighborhood" is wherever you find yourself at any given time. Everyone has a geographic neighborhood and several more relational neighborhoods— at work, the health club, the grocery store, a soccer game, our kids' schools, or any other place we regularly find ourselves with the same group of people. The principles we'll outline apply to those "neighborhoods," too.

WHAT HAPPENED TO THE OLD NEIGHBORHOOD?

You already know *how* neighborhoods have changed. To understand why hospitality and sociability have become so rare, we need to explore the *reasons* for this transformation.

A century ago, almost all neighborhoods were filled with families who lived there because the breadwinner worked close by. Some neighborhoods, especially in rural areas, retain this flavor today. Many, however, do not, largely because modern transportation makes commuting possible.

Social factors have played a huge role in changing neighborhoods, too. Divorce breaks up and disperses families. Intact families move more as job and career changes become more common. For more than a generation now, a higher percentage of mothers have been joining the workforce, meaning more houses are empty during the daytime.

Great numbers of people, both male and female, lack homemaking and hospitality skills. Many lack the time and energy needed; others simply never learned domestic skills because parents didn't model them. Remember the cookie-baking scenario we mentioned in the last chapter? That was real. Three girls in our neighborhood drop by our house sometimes and ask Becky to show them how to bake. That's because one day when she was baking, they came by to sell magazines for school playground equipment, and Becky invited them in. It turns out that baking is a foreign concept in their homes.

Cheryl Mendelson, in her excellent book *Home Comforts: The Art and Science of Keeping House*, summed up this condition:

> American housekeeping and home life are in a state of decline. Comfort and engagement at home have diminished to the point that even simple cleanliness and decent meals—let alone any deeper satisfaction—are no longer taken for granted in many middle-class homes. . . .
>
> Television often absorbs everyone's attention because other activities (such as music-making, letter-writing, socializing, reading or cooking) require at least a minimum of foresight, continuity, order, and planning that the contemporary household cannot accommodate. . . . These plagues rain on the lives of both rich and poor. Many people lead deprived lives in houses filled with material luxury.[2]

Even the "best" neighborhoods with the biggest, nicest houses are full of busy, tired, stressed people—Christians included—who know their home life lacks something that their parents or grandparents had.

Collectively, these factors account for most of the reasons people give for not extending more hospitality in their neighborhoods. That's a problem worth exploring.

With apologies to David Letterman, here are our top ten reasons why

Christians don't show hospitality to their neighbors:

10. I'm shy and introverted.

9. My house is too small.

8. My house is always a mess.

7. I couldn't bake a dozen cookies if my life depended on it.

6. I don't plan to live in this neighborhood very long, so why get attached?

5. I feel too embarrassed about not taking the initiative sooner to meet my neighbors. Now it's too late.

4. My neighborhood is already well-networked with lots of friendships among nonChristians whose lifestyles are much different from mine.

3. I don't have the spiritual gift of hospitality.

2. My spiritual life isn't all that great. I don't think God can use me in my present condition.

1. I barely have time for my own family, let alone my neighborhood.

Notice the common denominator in this list? Every one of them is me-centered.

Before we talk about how to reach out to neighbors, let us emphasize that your mindset and attitude are critical. Instead of dwelling on yourself and your fears, think of pleasing God and loving your neighbors.

Becky:

When I began to take seriously the fact that God was commanding me to love my neighbor as I love myself, I saw this hospitality thing as a matter of obedience. Then my focus shifted to pleasing Him, not myself.

Reaching out to my neighbors took on a whole new dynamic. I then discovered that my next-door neighbor was a new Christian who wanted to start a women's Bible study. I found another neighbor dying inside for kindness and attention from someone—anyone. Her husband had recently left her with two small boys to raise.

As I got out on my street and started being just a tiny bit friendly, God brought a whole bucket of needs to my attention. My heart began to fill with compassion for these neighbors. My prayer life became more purposeful and included neighbors by name. My joy increased as neighbors began to respond to my friendliness. When I wasn't thinking of myself and my own problems, all my excuses for not reaching out to neighbors began to dissipate. I began to look at people the way God does. ■

A CLOSER LOOK AT THE REASONS AND RATIONALES

If you agree that we're pretty close to identifying the top ten reasons people resist reaching out to those around them, they're worth investigating further. Let's dissect that list:

I'm shy and introverted. A lot of your neighbors are, too, or they would have reached out to you by now. So be shy and introverted together. Maybe you'll even grow. People are always waiting for someone else to make the first move, thinking their neighbors have things more together.

My house is too small. The question is, *How big is your heart?* We still hold summer block parties in our tiny driveway. We once hosted Christmas gatherings in a two-bedroom apartment with as many as seventeen people crammed into one small living room. A crowded room makes for a more exciting atmosphere in which people focus on each other, not on the house they're in.

My house is always a mess. All those TV channels and magazines featuring showcase homes are great, but that's media glitz and glamour. We'd like to see those spotless and sparkling abodes after the photographers leave! It might surprise you to know that people feel more comfortable visiting a lived-in house than one that looks like it belongs in *Better Homes & Gardens*. Think of how you feel touring a historic home. You're afraid to touch anything. You tiptoe around for fear of disturbing an exhibit. Of course, when you invite others in, the basic cleanliness of your home is important. But never let a messy house keep you from showing love to a neighbor.

I couldn't bake a dozen cookies if my life depended on it. Does that really matter? If you or your spouse can't make cookies, head down to the local bakery and buy some. Or show hospitality in another way. The important thing is not to let any feelings of embarrassment or shame about your home-making skills keep you from making a neighbor feel loved and wanted.

I don't plan to live in this neighborhood very long, so why get attached? As Christians, we are never in a place by accident—no matter how long we are there or whether or not we want to be there. In Jeremiah 29, the prophet addressed a nation of people who had prayed fervently that they wouldn't have to stay long in exile:

> This is what the LORD Almighty, the God of Israel, says to all those I carried into exile from Jerusalem to Babylon: "Build houses and settle down; plant gardens and eat what they produce.

Marry and have sons and daughters; find wives for your sons
and give your daughters in marriage, so that they too may have
sons and daughters. Increase in number there; do not decrease.
Also, seek the peace and prosperity of the city to which I have
carried you into exile. Pray to the LORD for it, because if it
prospers, you too will prosper." (verses 4-7)

In other words, bloom where you are planted.

*I feel too embarrassed about not taking the initiative sooner to meet my
neighbors. Now it's too late.* One of Satan's principal strategies is to accuse
and demean you for not being more spontaneous and open with your
neighbors. Don't fall for it. We have a friend who had lived in her neighborhood for a year before she decided to invite the neighbors over. The
two neighbors on either side of her had lived there *ten years* and had
never met before that day. You may have been slow to act, but others have,
too. You can end that problem for everyone.

*My neighborhood is already well-networked with lots of friendships
among nonChristians whose lifestyles are much different from mine.* Before
you even know your neighbors, you're accusing them of shutting you out.
You're assuming they don't want anything to do with you. That's probably not true. What's more, if there is already a network of friendships in
place, you won't have to start from scratch. You can join in, beginning
with the people you naturally like and enjoy.

I don't have the spiritual gift of hospitality. Ah, the Christian's ready-made
excuse. Let's make this point clear: At its most basic level, loving your
neighbor is not about individual gifts and talents. Jesus told us to love God

with all our heart, soul, strength, and mind and to love our neighbor as our-selves (see Luke 10:27). He didn't add, ". . . if that is your gift." Reaching out to those around you is simple obedience to God. It's a matter of caring enough for your neighbors to take a small risk. The apostle Paul couldn't be more clear and straightforward: "Practice hospitality" (Romans 12:13).

My spiritual life isn't all that great. I don't think God can use me in my present condition. If you admit your spiritual life needs help, congratula-tions for being so honest! And if God has made you aware of a particular sin, deal with it. Confess it to God, accept His forgiveness based on His promise in 1 John 1:9, and ask for the help and counsel of a mature Christian. But the fact is, you don't have to have all of your spiritual ducks in a row before God can use you. We are always in process. If you want to grow and mature in the faith, a good way to start is by loving your neighbor as yourself. You will develop a deeper walk with God as you reach out to others, because you will depend on Him more. Don't let any feeling of spiritual inadequacy keep you from obeying God.

I barely have time for my own family, let alone my neighborhood. Time— now there's a real obstacle to all of this. Amid running to and from work, school, and church activities, the neighborhood can become a pretty low pri-ority. But especially in the case of church activities, that problem deserves a closer look. We can't be so busy with other Christians, cloistered in our "holy huddle," that we don't plan any time for the nonChristians all around us.

In our family, we decided to make our neighborhood a priority. We attended one main church service a week and were active in a small group, but we didn't go to every church banquet, roller-skating party, and social function that was offered. All of those activities are well and good, but they wouldn't have left us time to just hang out in our neighborhood and interact with neighbors. We can't be so hurried and harried that we lose sight of what's important to God.

This is not just a time-management issue, at least in the way our culture has come to understand that term (which usually means learning to be more "efficient" so you can cram more activities into each day). Rather, think of time as manna, a daily resource provided by God and renewed with each new day. Consider what God would have you do with the time He gives you each day. Suddenly, your relationships with nonChristians will become a much larger priority, and some of those activities that have you running from appointment to appointment will pale in importance.

AN IRRATIONAL FEAR

Fear of extending hospitality is both a mental and spiritual condition. It's a real fear that can become a phobia—an irrational fear. God's Word promises that "perfect love drives out fear" and "God did not give us a spirit of timidity, but a spirit of power, of love and of self-discipline" (1 John 4:18; 2 Timothy 1:7). Confront your fears with God's Word, which clearly tells us that hospitality is not optional. The foundational truth of this book is this: The Great Commission is fulfilled when Christians live out the Great Commandment, "Love your neighbor as yourself." And hospitality is the outward expression of that love.

Taking that uncomfortable step of knocking on your neighbors' doors and inviting them over for coffee will begin to change your thinking and, more importantly, your heart. If this sounds difficult and scary, consider how you would feel if a neighbor extended you a hand of hospitality. You would be grateful he or she made the effort, and you would respond positively. In almost all cases, you will be pleasantly surprised to find your neighbors thrilled that you took that first step. Yes, people are busy and stressed, but they also long for a sense of community.

Becky:

I was trimming a bush by the garage one sunny, summer afternoon. My next-door neighbor Frank was working on a bush in his yard. We complimented each other on how nice the bushes were shaping up. One thing led to another, and I told him I had just baked rhubarb cobbler and he and his wife should come over for a bite to eat when she got home from work. He said, "I'm making stew in the Crock-Pot. I'll bring it over." We had a delightful supper, and as we were visiting in our living room, Frank said, "You know, we don't usually go to other people's houses like this. We kind of keep to ourselves. It's really neat to be here in your home."

It's important to mention that when you show hospitality, your neighbors may not reciprocate. Don't get discouraged. As Christians, we should not be motivated by the promise of repayment. We are servants. If you are the only one in your neighborhood obeying the Great Commandment, then your ministry is important indeed! ■

IDEAS FOR GETTING TO KNOW NEIGHBORS

Need a jump start in meeting your neighbors? Try these ideas:

- Sit outside in the evening on your front porch, driveway, or front lawn, where you may have contact with neighbors.

- Take walks around your neighborhood at times when folks are likely to be outside. Stop and talk when you get a chance. Add prayer to this exercise (more on this in chapter 5).

- If you know neighbors are going on vacation, offer to collect their mail or newspapers, bring in their trash cans, and keep an eye on their house.

- When a new family moves in, be the first neighbor to introduce yourself and bring over a pan of brownies or a loaf of homemade bread. Set up a time to have them over.

- Give new neighbors a 3 x 5 card containing your name, address, and phone number and invite them to call you with any questions about their new neighborhood.

- Put together a neighborhood directory of names, addresses, and phone numbers and give copies to all your neighbors.

- Babysit for your neighbors.

- Organize neighborhood service projects such as cleaning up litter, mowing common areas, raking leaves, helping a disabled neighbor with yard work or painting, and so on.

- Share clippings of plants (indoor or outdoor).

- If you bake, make extra cookies or pastries and give them to a neighbor.

- Invite one or two couples or individuals over for pizza or a barbecue and use the time to get acquainted.

- If a neighbor family has a new baby, take a meal. Offer baby clothes or accessories if you have them.

- When your child plays with other neighborhood kids, get to know their parents by inviting them over for dessert while the little ones have fun in the yard.
- Mow or rake your neighbors' lawn or shovel snow off their driveway or sidewalk.
- Help a neighbor build a deck, shed, gazebo, or swing set.
- Set up a car pool for trips to and from school, or wait at the bus stop with other parents.
- Visit a neighbor who is sick or hospitalized. This is one of the most powerful ways to show caring love.
- When neighbors stop by, invite them in—even when your house is a mess. Show them that their friendship is more important to you than keeping up appearances. Even if it's just a brief conversation, don't make them stand outside your door as you talk. That tacitly tells them you don't trust them.[3]

CONNECTING WITH A NEIGHBOR

Those first connections with neighbors often happen when you anticipate them and watch for opportunities. When we lived in Texas, we were walking to church one Sunday when we turned a corner and saw a couple working in their front yard. We said hello, and they were friendly in return. They asked where we were going, so we told them about our church and about ourselves. It wasn't a long conversation, but it ended with an invitation to church whenever they were interested. A few weeks later, they took us up on the offer. We also had them over to our house several times, and we became good friends. The husband and wife both eventually became Christians.

We could have walked right by them on that Sunday morning and not said a word. Making these connections is a matter of having your "radar" up. If you haven't decided that you will seek people out, and if you're not attentive to opportunities, then it probably won't happen. The Scriptures say that Jesus came to seek and save the lost. He was intentional.

Suppose you're walking down your street and you see a neighbor out mowing his lawn. He looks at you, so you smile and wave. As you get closer, he turns off the mower. If he were concentrating on his lawn and not making eye contact, you might choose to keep walking so you wouldn't bother him. But this time, he looks up again as if he wants to exchange a few words. A brief conversation ensues.

"Hi, it's good to see you. We haven't met. I'm Norm, from three houses down."

"I'm Steve."

"How long have you lived here?"

"Two years."

"We've been here about that long, too. Do you like the neighborhood?"

On it goes. Ask leading questions, and if you get feedback, proceed. If not, don't press. That's why Jesus asked people questions all the time — to see if they were open and receptive to further conversation. He was careful, just as we should be, not to be pushy or intrusive.

Another way to foster open communication with a neighbor is to offer a sincere compliment: "Your yard always looks great." An affirming comment makes people feel appreciated and important. They won't forget your kind words.

Also, remember not to get too personal right away. You don't want to come across as nosy. You probably know better than to say, "What was that police car doing in front of your house yesterday?" But at a first meeting, you may not even want to ask something as innocent as, "How long have you and your husband been married?" You can't assume couples living under the same roof *are* married. Besides, your neighbor may think, *What is it to you?* Keep things superficial initially and then move to more personal topics as you interact consistently and your comfort level with each other increases.

The following are three common questions we hear about reaching out to neighbors:

1. "What about neighbors who absolutely do not want to connect with anyone?" Don't force them. There will always be others who *do* want connections, and in them is where God is working.

2. "What if most of our neighbors are from a different ethnic group than our own? What if they are recent immigrants from another country and culture? What if there is a language barrier or a cultural barrier?" Reach out anyway. Try their food and take them yours. Food is a great catalyst for connection. It's an open door through which you can meet people. Keep in mind, too, that people from different cultures greatly appreciate it when someone makes an effort to reach out to them.

3. "What if we are the new family in the neighborhood? Doesn't protocol require that we not try to immediately become the neighborhood social organizers?" Have an open house to meet your new

neighbors a couple of weeks after you move in. Don't wait for them to make the first move. Often, they never will. It may be up to you to extend the hand of friendship. As Proverbs 18:24 tells us, "A man who has friends must himself be friendly" (NKJV).

All of these ideas are just common-sense principles for good communication. You're not following somebody else's script, like a telemarketer. Simply show genuine, natural interest and converse in a friendly manner. It will be your sincere acts of love and concern that touch a neighbor and attract him to Jesus.

Becky:

When Norm and I moved into our home in suburban Dallas, we decided to hold an open house. I was a nervous wreck. We'd lived there only three weeks, so we weren't close to being settled in. The real source of my nervousness, though, was in relating to these new neighbors. Because I grew up in a home that was full of criticism, I always felt inferior to everybody. As an adult, I felt that way in relation to women my own age, thinking they knew how to do everything better than I did. They were prettier than me, they had nicer clothes and finer furniture, and so on.

At the open house, we found out that one of our neighbors had broken a rib. To show my concern for her, I went over to her house one day to help with her toddler. She had the TV on, and an advertisement came on for *The Living Bible*. I asked her, "Do you like the Bible?" Her eyes lit up as she said she did and that she was a new Christian. It was such an exciting thing to find out that my next-door neighbor and her husband were Christians.

This young woman said she'd like to start a Bible study in the neighborhood. I responded enthusiastically, but my excitement faded slightly when she suggested that I should be the one to lead it.

I can remember arguing with the Lord: "Look at all the problems I have in my life, how stressed out I am most of the time, and what a bad mother I feel I am." Norm was busy with a new job and had many evening appointments, which added to the stress I already felt.

What I realized then is that the Lord doesn't wait for us to completely mature and get it all together before He decides to use us. He uses us in the midst of our own groaning and growing. It's really a matter of obedience, faith, and trust. God's power shows up most clearly in the weakness of people (see 2 Corinthians 12:9).

Despite the inferiority I felt among my new neighbors, a feeling of self-assurance always overshadowed my insecurity and doubt when I talked about my relationship with Christ and people responded. When we're willing to go an inch, God often takes us a mile. He gives and gives and gives, and it is He who does the work in people's lives! ■

Are you embracing God's command to love your neighbors? Is it a passion? Do you put forth conscious effort as you tend to those relationships? If not, ask God to give you that passion. And He will. Trust Him to arrange circumstances that will bring people across your path.

CHAPTER THREE

SEEING NEIGHBORS FROM GOD'S PERSPECTIVE

The Word became flesh and blood, and moved into the neighborhood.

JOHN 1:14, MSG

Thus far, we've talked about how we as Christians see and approach our neighbors. Have you ever stopped to think about how God views your neighbors? Two thousand years ago, we were given the perfect example.

For the better part of His first thirty years, Jesus lived in a neighborhood. Scripture says very little about His childhood, but there's no reason to believe He didn't grow up playing with other kids, and we can assume that as a young adult He worked and socialized with neighbors.

Jesus then spent His three-year ministry among the people—in neighborhoods and houses, at marketplaces and in the temple—tending to their physical and spiritual needs. John 1:14 in the *New American Standard Bible* says that Jesus "dwelt among us."

Think of another familiar Scripture from John's gospel: "For God so loved the world that he gave his one and only Son, that whoever believes in him shall not perish but have eternal life. For God did not send his Son

into the world to condemn the world, but to save the world through him"
(3:16-17). Put another way, God sought the lost by sending Jesus into the
world, which has always been made up of neighborhoods of some sort.
When Jesus left the earth, the Holy Spirit came to continue seeking the lost
in those neighborhoods. He does that through us, the body of Christ (see
Ephesians 5:30).

Scripture seems to come to life when we personalize it. We can apply
the concepts of John 1:14 and 3:16 and Ephesians 5:30 to ourselves this
way: God loved the people in a suburban Dallas subdivision. He wanted
to reach them, so He sent us into the neighborhood as Christ's ambassadors. We have come to realize that God "became flesh and blood, and
moved into the neighborhood" *through us!*

We encourage you to try this same exercise by filling in the following
blanks:

God loved (name of your neighborhood or community)
_____ so much that He sent (your name) _____
to reside on (name of street) _____ to live among
his/her neighbors as Jesus would, both in actions and words.

The apostle Paul tells us, "We are therefore Christ's ambassadors, as
though God were making his appeal through us" (2 Corinthians 5:20).
Indeed, God knows each of your neighbors intimately—every relationship, every struggle, every happy moment, every sin. Sure, He loves the
"safe" people. But He also loves the drug dealer down the street . . . and
that guy who has multiple tattoos and body piercings . . . and the couple

next door who hold the loud beer parties every weekend. He loves them so much that He sent His only Son to die for each one of them—and so much that He sent us to be His spokespersons. God does not want any of those neighbors to spend eternity apart from Him.

We must ask ourselves, *Do we want any of them to go to hell?* The Bible tells us, "[God] is patient with you, not wanting anyone to perish, but everyone to come to repentance" (2 Peter 3:9). Do you share God's sentiments toward your neighbors? Again, we encourage you to personalize that Scripture by completing the following exercises. We'll be talking about your geographic neighborhood, but you can also apply the activity to your relational "neighborhoods" (workplace, school, club, and so on).

PART ONE: ENVISIONING AN ETERNAL DESTINATION

On a piece of paper, draw your immediate neighborhood with its houses or apartments. Then list as many of your neighbors as you can think of. If you don't know their names, just describe something about them or their homes.

Mark a cross by those you believe may be Christians.

Mark an *X* by those you suspect, based on their words or lifestyles, are not Christians. (Yes, we realize this is speculation, as we can't see into another person's heart. But this is helpful in identifying who to reach out to with the gospel.)

Answer this question: Based on Scripture, if a person is not born again, where will that person go when he or she dies? Write that word next to those names with an *X* on your list.

This sounds harsh and judgmental, and you may feel uncomfortable doing it. Hell is a subject most people avoid thinking about. Picturing your neighbors there is even more discomforting. But we must agree with Scripture, not with our feelings or what a "tolerant" culture would say. We must see our neighbors through God's eternal perspective. Jesus died. Why? To rescue people from hell. He is the only way. As John 3:18 says, "Whoever believes in him is not condemned, but whoever does not believe stands condemned already because he has not believed in the name of God's one and only Son."

PART TWO: PERSONALIZING THE PROCESS

Now, take the names with an *X* on your list and insert them one by one in the blanks below:

The Bible says God does not want (neighbor's name)

_____ to perish. Do I want (neighbor's

name)_____ to perish? (yes/no). If no, what action

am I willing to take to give (person's name)

_____ an opportunity to go to heaven with

me? _____

    I will commit myself to pray for (neighbor's name)

_____, asking God to place me in situations where

Christ's life becomes evident through my words and deeds. I

will intentionally extend hospitality to (neighbor's name)

_____ through the following actions:

_____ within the following time
period: _____. This is my sincere and
prayerful goal.

A New Perspective

In Matthew 25, Jesus talks with His disciples about judgment:

> "For I was hungry and you gave me nothing to eat, I was thirsty
> and you gave me nothing to drink, I was a stranger and you did
> not invite me in, I needed clothes and you did not clothe me, I
> was sick and in prison and you did not look after me."
>
> They also will answer, "Lord, when did we see you hun-
> gry or thirsty or a stranger or needing clothes or sick or in
> prison, and did not help you?"
>
> He will reply, "I tell you the truth, whatever you did not
> do for one of the least of these, you did not do for me."
> (verses 42-45)

Now personalize the last line: "Whatever I did not do for (name any
neighbor) _____when I saw a need, I did not do for Jesus."

Wait a minute. How could God possibly expect us to meet the needs
of every hurting neighbor? No one could do that. Even Jesus didn't meet
every need when He walked the earth. The Word became flesh at one spot
on the map: Bethlehem. He dwelt among humankind in one place at a

time. During His whole earthly life, Jesus covered a distance of about 150 miles. He couldn't reach everyone, and God didn't expect Him to.

Yet when Jesus' earthly life was almost over, He said to God, "I have brought you glory on earth by completing the work you gave me to do" (John 17:4). Obviously, Jesus' supreme work was the Cross. But wouldn't He have felt frustrated or unfinished when there was so much He didn't have time to do, so many individuals He couldn't directly touch? No. He said that He had *completed* His work.

We are not capable of loving our entire neighborhood the way God does—becoming intimately involved in each person's day-to-day life. Nor does God expect that of us. In John 6:37, Jesus says, "All that the Father gives me will come to me, and whoever comes to me I will never drive away."

Jesus' parable of the Good Samaritan helps us see what God expects of us. A man was robbed, beaten, and left for dead. Two passersby looked the other way when they noticed him on the road. "But a Samaritan, as he traveled, came where the man was; and when he saw him, he took pity on him" (Luke 10:33).

Along our paths, God places the hungry, the thirsty, the homeless, the naked, the imprisoned—sometimes literally, most often figuratively. When we commit to truly loving our neighbors, we learn to look for opportunities to serve as God's ambassadors. If we ask Him, He will focus us on certain people like a laser beam and allow us to take their burdens from them.

Personalize Matthew 25 once again: If you saw needy, hurting people along your path this week and just kept on walking, you ignored Jesus.

Does that change the way you look at your neighbors and your role as a Christian? Wherever you live and whatever your circumstances, God has placed you in that position to allow Jesus to love your neighbors through you! His Spirit lives in you to do exactly that. While your goal may be to have a happy family and a comfortable home, it's important to realize that God has a larger, eternal purpose that extends beyond the needs of your own family.

It's a matter of living expectantly. In any situation, at any moment of any day, God might use you to show His love to someone. In an effort to be like Christ, you will be sensitive to that calling and obey it. A favorite old chorus goes like this: "Lord, lead me to some soul today and love that soul through me, and I will humbly do my part to win that soul to thee."

Norm:

One Thursday morning in mid-December 1995, I went to OfficeMax near our home in Littleton, Colorado, to buy some supplies. In an aisle stacked high with copy paper and manila envelopes, I overheard a conversation between two employees, both in their early twenties. One was saying how unhappy he was with his life. He was becoming more and more like his father, whom he didn't respect because of his drinking and bad temper. I overheard him say, "I am sick and tired of my dad coming home drunk and beating on my mom. He is ruining our Christmas. And the way I'm going, I'm afraid I'll end up just like him."

That last comment tugged at my heart, because when I was growing up, my own family situation had been similar. I sensed God wanting me to reach out to the clerk.

I approached him and said, "I overheard you talking to your friend there. I can relate to what you were saying."

I introduced myself, and he told me his name was Michael.

"You don't have to be afraid you will end up like your father," I told him. "I found that when I trusted in Jesus Christ and invited Him into my life, He changed me from the inside out. And I have been a new person ever since. He wants to do that for you, too."

Then I reached into my wallet and pulled out a copy of the *Four Spiritual Laws* booklet that I always carry with me. I told him briefly about how Christ could change his life and give him the assurance of heaven. He asked, "How is it possible to know for *sure* I'm going to heaven?" I knew he was on work time, so I cut the conversation short. But I asked if he would like to have breakfast sometime soon, and he said yes. We arranged to meet the following Sunday, his day off. I wrote my phone number on the back of the booklet, handed it to him, and encouraged him to read it carefully before we met.

About 9:30 on Sunday morning, I went to Michael's house to pick him up. Even though he lived in a nice, suburban neighborhood near Columbine High School, the house was unkempt and there was no phone. There was also no doorbell—just a hole where it was supposed to be—so I knocked several times. When no one answered, I knocked more loudly.

Finally, someone opened the door and said, "Come on in." I introduced myself, and he said, "Michael mentioned you were coming. He's probably sleeping downstairs."

As I walked downstairs, I was aware of beer bottles, the odor of drugs, and people sleeping on couches and the floor. I found Michael sound asleep in his bed with his head under the covers. When I woke him up, it took him a moment to remember me and our appointment. He apologized for forgetting and got up to take a quick shower. Soon, we were sitting across from each other at a nearby Village Inn restaurant.

As we ate, I asked Michael about his background. He'd been drinking and doing drugs since junior high, a total of about ten years. I realized quickly that this young man's life was a world away from what Becky and I knew, having raised two daughters who were following Christ. He recognized that, too, but still seemed comfortable with telling me some very personal things. Not only did he have a painful past, but he was now dealing drugs and running with a dangerous crowd. At times, I felt a little nervous, thinking, *God, why are you getting me involved with someone in this kind of lifestyle?*

But I kept talking, and he kept listening. Soon, I was going page by page with him through the *Four Spiritual Laws* booklet, explaining in simple terms the plan of salvation. As we reviewed the information and supporting Scriptures, I could tell that it was making sense to Michael.

Finally, I looked across the table at him and said, "God knows all about you and your past mistakes and lifestyle, and He wants to forgive you and come into your life as He did mine. Is there any reason that you would not like to pray and trust Christ to do in your life what He died to do?" And there at the Village Inn on that Sunday morning, Michael prayed and trusted Christ as his Savior.

I'd like to say that Michael's transformation was instantaneous—that his pain and misdeeds immediately became distant memories. In truth, he had a tough road ahead. He had prayed and received salvation, but his changes were only beginning. (We'll let Michael tell the rest of his incredible story in chapter 9.)

Where would Michael be today had I not obeyed the Holy Spirit and started that conversation at OfficeMax? I had plenty of good excuses not to: I was busy buying supplies for my office; he was working; I was much older than him and from a totally different walk of life. And where would Michael be today had I just gone to church that next Sunday morning as always instead of meeting him for breakfast? After all, I had given him the booklet and made him think. How much more should a Christian have to do?

I'm grateful that the Holy Spirit worked in my heart and prompted me to reach out to Michael as best I could. I'm pleased that I stepped out in faith, even though I wondered what in the world I was getting into. That's what the Lord wants: our obedient and loving response to His call. It's up to Him to do the rest. We just do whatever love would do and say whatever love would say, not something canned and programmed. ■

ISN'T IT ALREADY DECIDED?

Christians sometimes choose not to take a bold step and share Christ because they believe everyone's eternal destiny is already settled. Some Scriptures, such as Romans 8:29-30, certainly support the belief in predestination: "For those God foreknew he also predestined to be conformed to the likeness of his Son, that he might be the firstborn among many brothers. And those he predestined, he also called; those he called, he also justified; those he justified, he also glorified." Then there's Ephesians 1:11, which says, "In him we were also chosen, having been predestined according to the plan of him who works out everything in conformity with the purpose of his will."

So why worry about witnessing to your neighbors? Why be concerned about those people down the street who seem aloof and self-absorbed? Why talk to a stranger at OfficeMax? Doesn't God have everything sorted out already? The fact is, we can search the Bible and never find one verse that suggests we should withhold love and attention from those around us. Is a person who winds up never responding to Christ worth my time now? Of course! He's a person made in God's image; he's someone for whom Christ died. Christlike love does not just think in terms of the end results, of reaping a harvest.

As we suggested in the introduction, successful witnessing happens when Christians take the initiative to share Christ through the power of the Holy Spirit and leave the results to God. Christians often take too much responsibility for their neighbors' response to their hospitality and witness. But all God asks us to do is faithfully let Him love people through us.

If the concept of predestination is holding you back, think of it this way: We don't know who God has chosen and is pursuing. But we do know that He *is* choosing and pursuing specific people at specific moments in time. We also know that God has chosen to use us as His ministers of reconciliation. Therefore, out of obedience to the Great Commandment, we simply ask God to love people through us and to use us as His hands and mouth to help build His kingdom. Suddenly, every situation becomes a potential "divine appointment."

"FEED MY SHEEP"

The apostle Paul writes in Galatians 5:14, "The entire law is summed up in a single command: 'Love your neighbor as yourself.'" How do you love yourself? You first take care of yourself (and your family) in regard to basic needs: tangible ones such as food, clothing, and shelter and spiritual ones such as love for God and self-respect. Then you add cleanliness, health care, transportation. . . . The list goes on.

Are you willing to extend that kind of care to someone outside your family? To someone with whom you may not have anything in common? To someone who scares you? If you're totally honest with yourself, the answer is probably no—unless you've learned to change the focus of that question.

Let's imagine we have a next-door neighbor named George. It may not be very helpful to ask ourselves whether or not we love this fellow. If we're honest, we may answer that we *don't* really love him. In fact, we're not even sure we *like* him. This is not going to provide much motivation for witnessing to George. If we do show kindness to him, it might be out of guilt, which probably won't sustain our efforts for long. But here's the secret: Everything shifts when we focus on how much *God* loves George, what *God* thinks about him. We will then be motivated to reach out to George in love because we love God. Jesus gives us a model for this concept in John 21:15-18:

> When they had finished eating, Jesus said to Simon Peter, "Simon son of John, do you truly love me more than these?"
>
> "Yes, Lord," he said, "you know that I love you."
>
> Jesus said, "Feed my lambs."
>
> Again Jesus said, "Simon son of John, do you truly love me?"

He answered, "Yes, Lord, you know that I love you."

Jesus said, "Take care of my sheep."

The third time he said to him, "Simon son of John, do you love me?"

Peter was hurt because Jesus asked him the third time, "Do you love me?" He said, "Lord, you know all things; you know that I love you."

Jesus said, "Feed my sheep."

Jesus' choice of words is significant. He said, "Simon, do you love *me?* Then feed my sheep." He didn't ask if Peter loved the sheep.

God is still becoming flesh and moving into neighborhoods. As a Christian, you are the evidence. Many Christian leaders suggest that most people who come to faith in Jesus Christ do so because of the influence of a caring Christian friend or relative. The Great Commission will be fulfilled not primarily by professional clergy or evangelists but by believers who simply love their neighbors.

This chapter may have caused you to consider how God sees the people living around you. If so, that's terrific. And you may have been challenged to question whether or not you're loving people as our heavenly Father loves them. If you know you're not impacting your neighborhood the way God wants you to, either as an individual or as a family, then you may feel frustrated and guilty. As we'll see in the next chapter, that is the Holy Spirit's way of moving you toward a spiritual showdown.

CHAPTER FOUR

IT TAKES A FIGHT

The Spirit gives us desires that are opposite from what the sinful nature desires. These two forces are constantly fighting each other, and your choices are never free from this conflict.

GALATIANS 5:17, NLT

Picture a vintage professional wrestling show—the kind held in a smoky, dimly-lit amphitheater. A masked behemoth wins a match, then struts around the ring, daring anyone else to challenge him. The crowd boos and hisses, yet no one is brave enough to take him on.

Finally, an unlikely challenger climbs into the ring: a small, unknown guy. He looks like someone the giant could squash like a bug. The crowd laughs at first, then rallies behind the underdog. And in a hard-fought match between the good guy and the bad guy—surprise!—good triumphs.

That kind of drama may be a wrestling fan's fantasy, but it is, of course, based on a true story. Think back three thousand years to a valley in Judah. Goliath, the Philistines' nine-foot-tall warrior, has been trash-talking the entire army of Israel for forty straight days. Finally, a scrawny little contestant emerges: David. He can't believe what he is seeing and hearing and asks incredulously of Goliath, "Who is this uncircumcised Philistine that he should defy the armies of the living God?" (1 Samuel 17:26).

Then David climbs into the ring. You know the rest of the story.

A CONFRONTATION

We firmly believe that the question "Will you truly love your neighbor as yourself?" must move Christians to climb into the ring against formidable enemies: the world, our flesh, and Satan himself. Before our ministry of neighborly hospitality came about, we had to fight our way through invisible barriers of discouragement, guilt, accusation, resistance, and fear, both in our relationship as husband and wife and as uptight Christians.

In 1972, we lived in Anaheim, California. The two of us had driven home from a church activity late one spring evening. We parked our Buick in the driveway and paused. Through the car windows, we could see about twenty homes in our cul-de-sac, representing twenty sets of neighbors we knew but hadn't come close to reaching for Christ.

Our guilt and frustration hung over that street like a cloud worse than southern-California smog. We had lived in our neighborhood more than three years and had faithfully prayed for and befriended many neighbors, but we had been too fearful to mention the name of Jesus to even one of them. Very few had set foot inside our home.

Adding to our inner conflict, we had told ourselves that we were no "ordinary" Christians. We had our sights set on the mission field, already having spent the first year of our marriage in South America as missionaries-in-training. We both had graduated from Bible college, gone on short-term missions trips, attended evangelism seminars, and listened intently to countless sermons on overseas outreach. There was no questioning our desire to be Christ's witnesses. So this growing tension just didn't make sense. Obeying the command to "love thy neighbor" had been so natural as we slept on a dirt floor in Peru and shared Christ daily in the marketplace. Why did it seem so intimidating and elusive in our middle-class, suburban California neighborhood? We felt outside of God's will, like we were being disobedient Christians.

That night in the car, our frustrations boiled over into a shouting match. It's a good thing we had the windows closed so no one could hear our argument. We desperately wanted to reach out to our neighbors, but we had conflicting ideas about the approach we should take. We began accusing each other of not taking the lead.

Norm:

At the time, I was a regional sales manager for Encyclopedia Americana. Because of my temperament and training, I wanted to take a direct approach to telling our neighbors about Christ. Becky was secretly afraid I would go door-to-door handing out gospel tracts and asking our neighbors if they knew whether they were going to heaven or hell, just as we'd done in Peru. And I might have, just to unconsciously relieve my guilt. ■

Becky:

My approach was more subtle: Let's work harder at building relationships and living the Christian life, and someday a neighbor is bound to ask us how they, too, can become a Christian. I was afraid we would alienate the whole neighborhood if Norm started knocking on doors. ▪

Despite our different perspectives, we knew one thing for sure: Our approach of simply praying for our neighbors and waiting for God to move in their hearts wasn't having the desired impact. They probably saw that we were different, but for all we knew, they might have just thought we were religious people with whom they weren't likely to have a lot in common.

We ended that long, heated argument with a prayer: "Help, Lord. We don't know what to do. Please show us how to reach our neighbors and forgive us for being unkind to each other."

A week later, a friend invited us to a weekend Lay Institute for Evangelism conference put on by Campus Crusade for Christ in Arrowhead Springs, California. She even offered to take care of our two toddlers for the whole weekend. How could we refuse such an attractive offer?

At the conference, we hadn't even finished the first seminar when we looked at each other and said together, "Thank you, Lord, for answering our prayer." Sure, there was practical advice about sharing our faith—how to use a booklet such as the *Four Spiritual Laws,* steer a conversation toward the gospel, do a "heart check" on ourselves for obedience, repentance, and cleansing of sin. But the conference taught us that the real focus of evangelism is much simpler than we'd imagined. Christians need to take the initiative to share Christ in everyday situations, depend on the power of the Holy Spirit, and leave the results to God. It doesn't mean going door-to-door with tracts, nor does it mean merely praying that our neighbors will see Christ in us. It means that we are to lovingly engage them without worrying about how they will respond. Simply put, there is no impact without contact.

Back home from the conference with a new focus, we began to see opportunities to express Christ's love to our neighbors, opportunities that had been right under our noses. A week later, our babysitter, whom we'll call Ashley, stopped by to thank us for a graduation gift we had given her.

Norm:

I began asking her about her future, and she said she wasn't sure what she wanted to do. I asked if she had included God in her plans.

"Have you ever heard of the *Four Spiritual Laws* booklet?" I asked. "It's helped us in our life and in our decision making. It might be a help to you, too. Can we read it with you?"

She said yes. I read through the booklet, stopping occasionally to explain various points. About twenty minutes later, Ashley bowed her head and prayed with us as she received Christ.

Later, as Ashley walked across the street toward home, Becky and I felt that proverbial cloud of guilt finally starting to lift. The sun—or in this case, the Son—had started to shine in our neighborhood. ■

The Campus Crusade conference had included the idea of having a neighborhood Christmas party where Christians, in a nonthreatening environment, could share their hope in Christ. The following December, we decided to try it. Obstacles sprang up. In fact, we almost canceled the party ten days beforehand when our cohosts, another Christian couple, backed out. They thought the idea was too aggressive. Our old fears and hesitations came back in full force. But we stuck to the resolve we had reached earlier that year.

Norm:

To our amazement, about twenty neighbors came to our party. It was exciting to finally have them in our home. We enjoyed holiday food, played games, and sang Christmas carols. Everyone was relaxed and sociable. Toward the end of the evening, I asked each guest to share a favorite Christmas memory or how they came to know the real meaning of Christmas.

Finally, my turn came. Despite a dry mouth and extreme nervousness, I talked about growing up in snowy Minnesota, how we used to celebrate Christmas with a lot of tensions, and how all of the first-born males on my father's Swedish side of the family were given the middle name Emmanuel, which means "God with us." I told how my mom had accepted Christ with a visiting pastor and how I had been next, followed by my sister and brother. I ended my talk by handing out and explaining the *Four Spiritual Laws* booklet, fighting fears that it might bring the party to an awkward close.

Our neighbors' response caught us off guard. The group seemed completely comfortable with my openness. A couple of people spoke up, mentioning the churches they attended. One woman sitting on the piano bench said that she had just become a Christian a few months earlier and was happy to find this was "such a Christian neighborhood."

Within a month, a women's Bible study had started in our neighborhood. Two months after that, three women in the group had accepted Christ. We thought, *This is amazing!* We'd been there three-and-a-half years, feeling guilty, afraid, and uptight, not knowing what to say or how to say it. Then we'd resolved simply to be open and loving. Now, within just a few months, great things were happening.

Thus began an adventure that, several neighborhoods and more than thirty years later, continues to amaze us. Even if you are actively sharing Christ with people in your workplace or elsewhere, nothing compares to sharing Christ with a neighbor. That touches the fiber of our souls because it hits closer to home and we can see the impact every day. But it will not happen without a fight. ■

A NEW IDENTITY

The book of Genesis features an account of one of the most intriguing wrestling matches of all time:

> Jacob was left alone, and a man wrestled with him till day-
> break. When the man saw that he could not overpower him,
> he touched the socket of Jacob's hip so that his hip was
> wrenched as he wrestled with the man. Then the man said,
> "Let me go, for it is daybreak."
>   But Jacob replied, "I will not let you go unless you bless me."
>   The man asked him, "What is your name?"
>   "Jacob," he answered.
>   Then the man said, "Your name will no longer be Jacob,
> but Israel, because you have struggled with God and with men
> and have overcome." (32:24-28)

Many biblical scholars believe Jacob wrestled with the Lord Himself that night. Afterward, his spiritual identity changed, from Jacob (which means "He grasps the heel") to Israel ("He struggles with God"). That name change is significant for Christians today. We believe that in order to cross the line from *knowing* to *doing,* we each have to win a wrestling match in our soul—a fight that will change our spiritual identity.

Norm:

My fight resulted in a total change in spiritual focus. I articulated my new mission in this way: "From now on, I will take the initiative to share Christ when I see the opportunity or when the Holy Spirit urges." Before, as I talked with a person, the thought to share Christ would occur, but the opportunity would come and go as I consciously questioned my "impressions." Now, there's no question about whether or not I should share Christ immediately when I recognize the opportunity. ■

Becky:

I gained some insights through our argument and the subsequent answer to our prayer for help that night. First, God loves my neighbors more than I do. I knew that by the way He was burdening my heart for them. Second, He has already given me the command to love them and tell them the good news. Third, the missing ingredient was simply my obedience to that command. And fourth, when I choose to obey His command, God works simultaneously and brings many of my neighbors to Himself. Seeing my neighbors embrace Christ has been the single greatest joy of my life. ■

UNCOMFORTABLE QUESTIONS

Imagine sitting in church and hearing the pastor ask the congregation, "What is the most important thing that has ever happened to you?"

You respond, "Accepting Christ as my personal Savior."

Then he asks, "What is the most important thing you could ever do to show love to your nonChristian neighbor?"

Obviously, the majority of the church members, including yourself, answer, "Share the gospel with them so they can find Christ, too."

Then the pastor asks a third question: "How many of you have done that in the last week? Month? Year? Five years?"

There's an uncomfortable pause. People glance around the room. Very few hands go up. Why? If it's so clear to us as Christians that God wants us—and commands us—to share Christ with our neighbors, why do so many of us choose not to?

One reason is that we are in a spiritual battle and are reluctant to engage nonbelievers. Envision a wrestling ring again. We know one opponent, Satan, is already prowling around "like a roaring lion looking for someone to devour" (1 Peter 5:8). Many of us Christians decide not to enter the ring. We choose to ignore all those nosy questions the pastor asked. We compare ourselves to gifted evangelists and say, "I could never do that. Surely, God doesn't expect that of me."

Every time we shrug off the responsibility of telling our neighbors about Christ, our enemy, Satan, wins. Are we content with that? Or does that motivate us to enter the ring? Joshua 24:15 puts the struggle in plain terms: "If serving the LORD seems undesirable to you, then choose for yourselves this day whom you will serve. . . . But as for me and my household, we will serve the LORD." We want that last phrase to be our motto and mission for life.

OVERCOMING RESISTANCE

In chapter 2, we listed the top ten excuses Christians give for not showing neighborly hospitality. Now let's look at the top ten reasons Christians don't share Christ with their neighbors. As you read through these, consider which ones apply to you:

10. I don't know my neighbors well enough to get personal.

9. I'm afraid I'll look like a fanatic and alienate them.

8. I wouldn't know what to say. I'm not knowledgeable and articulate enough about my faith to share it with others.

7. I'm introverted. I have enough trouble starting *any* conversation with a neighbor, let alone one about spiritual issues.

6. I've tried before and flopped. My neighbor quickly changed the subject and hasn't talked to me much since then.

5. There's too much sin in my life. Every time I feel led to share my faith with a neighbor, I realize I'm a lousy advertisement for Christianity.

4. I don't want to think of my neighbors as spiritual "projects." I'd feel like a salesperson, and they would see through it.

3. It would take time and energy that I just don't have. I'm involved in other ministries that are more suited to my spiritual gifts.

2. I don't think fast enough on my feet. I want opportunities, and they sometimes pop up, but I don't recognize them until it's too late.

1. It's a big enough challenge just trying to keep my own kids on the right path. Who's got time for the whole neighborhood?

Notice that, just like our list in chapter 2, all of these reasons focus on *self*, and most begin with "I." Many Christians fail to reach out to neighbors because they are centered not on their neighbors, but on themselves. Now let's examine those top ten reasons:

I don't know my neighbors well enough to get personal. We can't love our neighbors as ourselves unless we first *know* them. So, it stands to reason that God expects us to obey Him and befriend our neighbors. (Refer back to chapter 2 for suggestions on how to do this.)

I'm afraid I'll look like a fanatic and alienate them. Love for your neighbors will remove this objection because there is no fear in love. The gospel may indeed be offensive, but your mannerisms need not be. Yes, there's still a risk neighbors might see you as a fanatic. But then again, maybe they won't. Which is more important—avoiding risk or obeying God?

I wouldn't know what to say. I'm not knowledgeable and articulate enough about my faith to share it with others. You don't need to be a Bible scholar or a skilled orator. Just be yourself! Try writing your testimony. How did you come to Christ? Remember, it's not knowledge that attracts people to Christ—it's love. A contagious, childlike faith does not require a divinity degree.

I'm introverted. I have enough trouble starting any conversation with a neighbor, let alone one about spiritual issues. Even the apostle Paul prayed for boldness. Dr. Bill Bright, founder of Campus Crusade for Christ, used to say he had rarely shared the gospel with someone without experiencing a conscious internal fight. Sure, there's the issue of temperament; some people are more verbal and outgoing than others. But even the shyest among us can, when necessary, discuss potentially awkward issues with people they love or care about. Love takes us beyond our natural barriers, and the Holy Spirit gives us both the courage and the words we need.

I've tried before and flopped. My neighbor quickly changed the subject and hasn't talked to me much since then. If you've tried and failed, consider yourself in good company. The most skilled and effective evangelists could tell you their own discouraging tales. Congratulate yourself for trying and know that next time you'll do better. Research shows that the average person who finally responds to the gospel has had about six previous exposures. Your neighbor may have changed the subject, but you don't know the struggle that may be going on in his or her soul. Continue to respond in love and care, and leave the results to God.

There's too much sin in my life. Every time I feel led to share my faith with a neighbor, I realize I'm a lousy advertisement for Christianity. We must deal with personal sin first or we'll never reach the main event—the fight for others' souls. Hebrews 12:1 begs us to "throw off everything that hinders and the sin that so easily entangles." In the next chapter, we'll show you one method of doing this. For now, understand this: There may, in fact, be issues in your life that must be addressed. There may be failures you need to confront and confess. But if you are waiting for your life to be spotless and pristine before you'll share your faith with neighbors, accept that it will never happen. God delights in using imperfect people to accomplish His purposes. Jesus taught that those who accept the most forgiveness are the very ones who show the most love (see Luke 7:36-50).

I don't want to think of my neighbors as spiritual "projects." I'd feel like a salesperson, and they would see through it. You're right. They are not projects, and they are not the enemy. They are the victims of the Enemy. A salesperson makes a sale for his or her own benefit. You, as an ambassador for Christ, are simply passing on the hope that was given to you.

It would take time and energy that I just don't have. I'm involved in other ministries that are more suited to my spiritual gifts. It's vital that every believer serves in a manner consistent with his or her spiritual gifts. But when Jesus gave the Great Commandment, He implied that we—meaning all of us—are to take time to obey it. Loving your neighbor as yourself is every Christian's responsibility. It is not dependent on any spiritual gift.

I don't think fast enough on my feet. I really do want opportunities, and they sometimes pop up, but I don't recognize them until it's too late. That's a very common objection. We suggest that you memorize a few transitional sentences to steer a friendly, everyday conversation toward the gospel. Here are some that have helped us:

- I'm curious—do you have a religious background?
- We're really enjoying the church we belong to. Do you attend church anywhere?
- Do you have any spiritual beliefs?

This may turn you off as sounding rehearsed, but we ask these questions sincerely. We've found that if we don't have questions like this ready, we can be caught off guard by an opportunity and not say anything. Compose your own transitional sentence to use in addition to these.

It's a big enough challenge just trying to keep my own kids on the right path. Who's got time for the whole neighborhood? The answer for us has been to look at individual opportunities, not the entire neighborhood. We do pray for the whole neighborhood, but then we watch for God's direction. He makes it obvious when He wants us to say something. Thinking about winning every one of your neighbors to Christ is intimidating and unrealistic, but the goal becomes much more manageable when you focus on one person at a time. And after many months or years, you may, in fact, have touched your whole neighborhood.

SYMPTOMS AND SOLUTIONS

We've just picked apart our invisible opponent's strategy against us. Not one of those reasons stands up as having come from God. In fact, they directly oppose what He tells us in Scripture. Are you content to hide behind invalid objections, or are you ready to engage your opponent in a fight?

Years ago in Anaheim, our guilt level got so high we couldn't stand it anymore. Sure, we fought with each other about our different ideas, styles, and approaches. We felt frustrated and discouraged. But those were just symptoms of what was going on in each of us spiritually. We both were losing our fights because we had not decided that we *would* fight. Most Christians have chosen not to get involved because they assume that winning depends on them rather than on the true victor, the Spirit of God.

It's okay to have that struggle. There's no avoiding it if you are truly committed to following Christ. If it happens with one or both partners in a marriage, it can cause the same kind of anger and dissension we felt. You'll have to work through tough questions: "Have we decided to obey the first and greatest commandment?" Only then will we truly desire to love our neighbor as ourselves. "Do we love God so much that we will reach out to those around us?" That is the essence of the fight.

CHAPTER FIVE

PRAYER: LAYING THE FOUNDATION

Brothers, my heart's desire and prayer to God for the Israelites is that
they may be saved. ROMANS 10:1

When you chose your present home, did you pray about the decision? Most Christians would answer yes. But did you pray simply for the best place for you and your family? For the most comfortable home? For the best investment? Or did you also pray for your potential neighbors and the relationships that lay ahead?

When a Christian individual, couple, or family moves into a neighborhood, so does Jesus. We have new neighbors and a new chance to obey His command to love our neighbor as ourselves. To be sure, God thinks of our practical needs when we move from one home to another. But He also has the spiritual needs of the neighborhood in mind. He is always seeking and saving the lost, and He does that through believers.

Our enemy, Satan, is also thinking about those things and trying to thwart us. He maintains strongholds—sin, hard-heartedness, pain, despair—in the lives of those around us. In such a spiritual battle, there is necessary groundwork to be laid for reaching our neighbors: prayer.

About a year after "the fight" in Anaheim, we were transferred to the Dallas area to work with Campus Crusade for Christ. We asked our former neighborhood Bible study group and church to pray for us—that God would pick the house and the neighborhood where He could use us again to share Christ. This time we weren't going to wait three-and-a-half years to start investing in lives.

We left Anaheim with mixed emotions. Why would God move us at that particular time? We had just begun to experience His miraculous work in our neighborhood. But once we did move, we became very conscious of our new neighbors. With great expectation, we believed we would connect with some of them and they would come to Christ.

One of the first evenings in Richardson, we took a walk around our cul-de-sac, praying for our neighbors. We almost bumped, literally, into a neighbor who was stumbling around, drunk as a skunk. That encounter became symbolic of the spiritual darkness that would surround us as we launched a ministry in new territory.

The same may be true for you as you commit to reaching your neighbors. Before we talk about how to plan parties, share testimonies, start Bible studies, and more, let's be clear: None of that will be effective without a solid foundation of prayer.

In the fall of 2001, our friends John and Sharon Marquis, along with their three children, moved into a neighborhood in Evergreen, not far from our present Colorado home. We'll let them tell you how prayer impacted that neighborhood.

John and Sharon:

When we moved from a Denver suburb to the mountains, we felt strongly that there was a reason we ended up in this house. We'd liked the house but hadn't expected to be able to afford it. We made a very low offer in our opinion, but the sellers' counteroffer fell within our price range.

Soon, the house was ours—well, sort of. From the beginning, we knew God had provided this house for us, and we said, "Okay, Lord, we're dedicating this house to you and to your work. We're a light on a hill here. However you can use us, please do that." ■

Sharon:

God quickly started answering that prayer. Becky and I were leading a ladies' Bible study on Tuesdays. The topic was evangelism, which I've always had a heart for. The "final exam" for that fall course was to host a neighborhood outreach Christmas party. I felt pretty excited about that. ■

John:

I felt intimidated. We had just moved into the neighborhood and hadn't even met anybody yet. I thought, *This seems a little early to go out and evangelize the neighbors. Maybe we should get to know them first.* But Sharon and I decided that a Christmas party would be an excellent way to get acquainted.

We decided to have a "pre-evangelistic" party, a nonthreatening way to build bridges and form relationships. Christ definitely would be a part of the evening, but there would not be a formal invitation to respond to the gospel. Our planning began with prayer, and then we took the first step of faith— delivering the invitations. ■

Sharon:

I'd been learning more about prayer in the midst of all this. It's really the starting point for effective evangelism. I started "prayer walking" (and sometimes prayer *driving*) through my neighborhood, which means strolling through the streets and praying for each home and family individually without necessarily knowing specific needs. I'd been reading Ron Hutchcraft's book *Called to Greatness*, which makes the point that evangelism is not just talking to a person about God—it's first talking to God about that person and then asking God to show us what He has for us to do. ■

John:

We spent a lot of time in prayer for this party, not only that people would open up, but also for the right words to say. We wanted people to feel the love of Jesus. This was a real step of faith for me, considering that I am not very outspoken or evangelistic and didn't even know these people.

Because our new house was fairly large, we'd invited about sixty people, thinking maybe half of those would actually come. But fifty came! Our house was packed. And God did give us the words to say. He provided the comfort of being able to interact with our guests.

The central event of the party was a time of sharing favorite holiday memories. We were surprised that several neighbors talked openly about how Christmas meant the love of Christ and how important that was to them.

Some of the neighbors who hadn't seemed outspoken at first started contributing to the conversation. We could feel the Lord creating warmth and love in that room as Christians and nonChristians alike shared their fond memories in such a loving way. There were a lot of teary-eyed people in that room.

That was powerful for me, and I think *they* thought it was powerful, too.

Our party planted seeds for friendships and further opportunities to share Christ with several neighbors. We know that it never would have been successful without prayer. When you see others praying for your party and friends willing to prayer walk in your neighborhood, it's a beautiful vision of the body of Christ working together. You see God's fingerprints on every little detail. ■

LOOKING INWARD FIRST

Deciding to make yourself completely available to God for the sake of your neighbors is no casual choice. In fact, it's a good idea to begin with a sincere commitment in prayer or a written declaration. We offer the following as a template, which you can adapt to your situation.

> Dear heavenly Father,
>
> I choose to accept that beyond loving you with all my being, my main purpose in life is to "love my neighbor just as I love myself." You called this the Royal Law, saying that all other commands concerning my relationships with people are based on my fulfilling this one law. That means I will take the initiative to befriend, love, and care for those around me. I will do what I can to help them understand the gospel message and trust in Christ.
>
> I pray you would grant me the awesome privilege of assisting many to accept your love and forgiveness in Christ. I

will use my gifts and abilities to that end. I realize that every man, woman, and child I meet is made in your likeness and is therefore worthy of my unconditional love. I look forward to your leading.

Your son/daughter, _____

Date: _____

Next, ask God to examine your life. As the apostle Paul wrote to the believers in Philippi, "Whatever happens, conduct yourselves in a manner worthy of the gospel of Christ" (Philippians 1:27). Be sure there is no unconfessed sin in your life. You might want to pray the words of Psalm 139:

Search me, O God, and know my heart;

test me and know my anxious thoughts.

See if there is any offensive way in me,

and lead me in the way everlasting. (verses 23-24)

As God reveals your wrongdoing, humbly and contritely seek the Lord's forgiveness, saying something like this: "Father, I agree with you that I have fallen short of your standard in this area, and I ask for your mercy and grace. I now accept your forgiveness for that specific sin. I accept your promise that you will 'cleanse [me] from all unrighteousness'" (1 John 1:9, NKJV). You are free! You have consciously accepted God's forgiveness, granted through Jesus' death on the cross, for every specific sin you are aware of. This is how we become clean vessels for God to use. Once you have settled the sin issue, things will start to happen.

The psalmist wrote,

> Blessed is he
>> whose transgressions are forgiven,
>> whose sins are covered.
> Blessed is the man
>> whose sin the LORD does not count against him
>> and in whose spirit is no deceit. (32:1-2)

Ask for and accept by faith the power and control of the Holy Spirit over every area of your life. God promises to give it to you because it is His will (see 1 John 5:14-15). Of course, defeating sin is no one-time struggle. Dr. Bill Bright of Campus Crusade for Christ likens the continuing process to spiritual breathing. We *exhale* by confessing our sins to God. We then *inhale* by accepting by faith His forgiveness and filling of the Holy Spirit.

One of Satan's chief strategies is to use guilt and shame to make Christians feel unworthy and inadequate. Remember, God uses us not according to our ability, but our availability. Human history is full of examples of God using imperfect people who are fully dependent on Him.

Be prepared for spiritual battles. God's Word is clear that you will face spiritual opposition when you decide to obey Him, especially when souls are at stake. As James 4:7 tells us, "Resist the devil, and he will flee from you." And Ephesians 6:11 says, "Put on the full armor of God so that you can take your stand against the devil's schemes."

What kinds of schemes can you expect? Anything and everything. The furnace goes on the fritz. The car breaks down. Health problems, marital stress, scheduling conflicts, strong temptations in your weakest areas . . . anything that can distract you from loving others.

These are the "flaming arrows of the evil one" that Paul describes in Ephesians 6:16. Don't fear them and don't be surprised by them. Pray against them daily and ask others to do the same. This is war—war for people's souls. When the enemy is cornered and overmatched, he fights back with everything he can.

Becky:

In Richardson, we were going to have a June pool party for the couples in our neighborhood. Many of the women had been coming to my Bible study. Several were new Christians, but most of their husbands still were not. One of the husbands invited three couples who were planning on attending the pool party to go out to eat on the very same night. We strongly suspected that this man was trying to "run interference" and undermine our efforts. My friend called and said, "We have a spiritual battle going on. Satan is trying to keep these couples from coming to the party. We need to pray."

We did, and we asked others in the Bible study to pray as well. The man who was working against us didn't come to the party and neither did his wife. But nobody went with them to dinner, either, and two of the couples who had been invited came to our party instead. Within the next couple of months, one of the husbands and one of the wives accepted Christ. So out of that spiritual battle, we saw two people come to know the Lord.

When spiritual battles intensify—and they will—remind yourself of 1 John 4:4: "The one who is in you is greater than the one who is in the world." God wants us to depend on Him, not on our own strength. We do that by praying and by realizing that God has allowed this battle. ■

MOVING FORWARD

Earlier in this book, we asked you to think about each home in your neighborhood and to pray for your unsaved neighbors, asking God to place you in situations where Christ becomes the topic of conversation. Hopefully, you committed to extending hospitality to specific neighbors by doing specific things within a specific period of time. Now what?

Sharon Marquis has already mentioned the power of prayer walking through your neighborhood. It's a great way to begin following through on those commitments. We'll let Sharon's prayer partner from our evangelism class, Pat Johnston, tell you about her experience.

Pat:

My husband, Ralph, and I have lived in our neighborhood in Morrison, Colorado, for twenty-six years. When the kids were younger and in school, we knew the neighbors very well. But once all three of our kids graduated and moved on, we started losing contact with those who lived around us. There weren't any neighborhood activities to keep us connected.

I took a class on evangelism a few years ago but never really did much with it. Then, more recently, I took the evangelism class taught by Becky and Sharon. Our assignment was to have a party with our neighbors to get to know them and perhaps even start a Bible study. So I planned a spring party for the women in my neighborhood.

Before the party, Sharon and I did a prayer walk through my neighborhood. As we walked down the street, we prayed for each neighbor and talked a little about each one. We prayed for specific concerns if we knew them and if not, we just prayed in general. We asked God to create opportunities to get acquainted and inspire interest in a Bible study.

Along the way, we met a young woman who was moving in with her boyfriend. As we talked and told her about the party, she and Sharon really seemed to connect. She was excited to meet new neighbors.

We ended up having a successful party. Of those we personally invited, about twenty-five women came, and the relationships formed there were a first step toward sharing Christ with them. In fact, the young woman we met as we were walking is now one of several from our party involved in a neighborhood Bible study.

I don't think I would have had the courage to go through with the party if Sharon and I hadn't spent so much time in prayer beforehand. You have to have a passion for your neighborhood and a desire to do something different. My prayer was that God would give me more passion in my life. That's why I took the evangelism class. It was a stretch for me, and I could have been scared off, I guess. But I'd reached the point where I knew that just *learning* about evangelism is not enough. Actually doing it—and bathing the process in prayer—is what counts. ■

HOW TO PRAY FOR YOUR NEIGHBORS

Prayer walking allows you to focus on each house and each family as you stroll past. If a neighbor is outside, it's a great opportunity to strike up a conversation. Because you're in an attitude of prayer, you may have a heightened sensitivity to your neighbors' spiritual needs.

Another method that's being used nationwide follows the acronym BLESS.[4] This can be used instead of prayer walking or as a supplement to it. You can use it to guide your prayers for neighbors.

Body: Pray for their health needs.

Labor: Pray for their job/work needs.

Emotional: Pray for their emotional needs.

Social: Pray for their relationships with family and friends.

Spiritual: Pray for their salvation.

Whatever approach you take, the important thing is that you develop a method to faithfully pray for your neighbors. You might begin by making a list of neighbors and then praying for them according to your favorite Scriptures. For example, Becky often prays the words of Acts 26:17-18, where Jesus said to Paul, "I am sending you to them to open their eyes and turn them from darkness to light, and from the power of Satan to God, so that they may receive forgiveness of sins and a place among those who are sanctified by faith in me." Your prayer might be, "Lord, please use me as I reach out to (neighbor's name). Open his/her eyes to your light and love. Overcome Satan and enable my friend to have an open heart to receive your grace and forgiveness through knowing Jesus Christ."

Some people keep prayer lists in their wallets or purses, on the car dashboard, or in a guest book. We even know families who write neighbors' names on slips of paper in a bowl that's kept at the dining room table. At mealtime, they draw a name and pray for that person.

DON'T GO IT ALONE

Even if yours is the only Christian home on your street, you will be far from alone in your efforts if you involve your church family. One of the most exciting ways the body of Christ can work together is by praying for each other's neighbors.

In Richardson, our church included a share-and-prayer time during the Sunday morning service. Often, we would mention someone in our neighborhood we were reaching out to and that person would be prayed for on the spot. The members of our congregation would often see the results of those prayers a few weeks later when we brought that neighbor to church. Other believers in our church became encouraged by this to reach out to their neighbors. Each week as we shared prayer requests and answers together, the whole church eagerly anticipated what God was going to do.

Loving your neighbors need not be an individual effort because we are connected to the family of God. As we share our neighbors' needs with our church and with other Christian friends, we gain courage, knowing that people are praying with us. Hebrews 10:24 says, "Let us consider how we may spur one another on toward love and good deeds." As Christians, we have a mission together—to love our neighbors and tell them the good news of Jesus Christ. Let's join together and pray together, so we can see God perform miracles in our neighborhoods.

CHAPTER SIX

PLANNING A NEIGHBORHOOD PARTY

It's like you're going to the greatest party ever and get to invite anyone you want.

DAN AND DAVE DAVIDSON AND GEORGE VERWER, *GOD'S GREAT AMBITION*

Sharing Christ through neighborly hospitality is often a matter of spontaneous and serendipitous meetings. But in a busy neighborhood where chance encounters are all too rare, sometimes your efforts must be intentional and deliberate. We have found that the best way to help neighbors get to know one another beyond the "smile and wave" level of friendship is to host a neighborhood party. Christmas, the Fourth of July, or any other occasion throughout the year will work. And at that party, the love of Christ can be extended.

To show you the typical process of planning and hosting an evangelistic neighborhood party, we'll introduce you to our friends Bert and Lisa Wycoff. They're a couple in their early thirties who moved to Littleton in 2000 with their three children (they've since added twins).

Lisa:

On September 11, 2001, our church kicked off a series of Tuesday morning women's Bible studies. I went to the study I had signed up for but quickly realized I should have joined a different one—the one on evangelism. With the terrible events going on that day, I felt an urgent desire to reach out to my neighborhood, especially a particular neighbor for whom I felt a real burden.

I knew Becky had been scheduled to lead the evangelism class, so I called and asked if she had any openings in it. She said nobody had signed up for her study, so she wasn't going to do it this year. I said, "What? You *have* to lead this study because I have a neighbor who needs Jesus and I need to learn more about this stuff."

Well, Becky and her coleader, Sharon, prayed about it and decided to take me on as their only student. In the class, I memorized Scripture and learned techniques for sharing my faith. The final assignment was to host a neighborhood Christmas party. I was scared to death. We had lived in our neighborhood for just a year and a half, and we still didn't know many people. Fortunately, the neighborhood is very social, and each year families take turns hosting a Christmas party. We had gone to it the year before. People were drinking, and the conversations were very shallow and gossipy. But even then we knew it was important to make contact with our neighbors.

After learning about the party I was to host, I went home to share all of this with my husband. ■

Bert:

When I found out this party was to be evangelistic, my first reaction was fear at how the neighbors would react. It's easier to evangelize when it's not in your neighborhood because you don't have to see the people all the time. If you witness to somebody and he turns you down, well, that's his decision and you move on. But when it's your neighbors, you have to live with knowing how they responded, and you wonder what they're going to say to your other neighbors on the block.

I've always been inclined toward evangelism, but this was a big step. It seemed a lot riskier, and there was more at stake. We live just a few blocks from Norm and Becky, so they popped over one night to talk about this. I didn't need to be convinced that evangelism is important or that it's a call for every Christian. I knew that. But I had an internal struggle going on about actually hosting a get-together.

Norm and Becky have an enthusiasm and spirit that are contagious. It was their experience with hosting parties and their excitement about it that gave me the confidence to go forward. They pointed to Scripture, which always gives me a kick in the seat. We're not called to protect our image or to protect the things the Lord has given us. We're called to be servants, and that involves His agenda, not ours. ■

Lisa:

We were excited that someone was challenging us right at the moment we needed it. In October, I called the neighborhood "mediator"—the person who seems to know everybody's business—and told her that Bert and I would love to host the Christmas party this year. She said, "Great! Nobody else has stepped up to the plate yet."

Our handmade invitations told the date and time for the party, asked people to bring a favorite holiday dish, and said that friends of ours would share inspirational thoughts about "the true meaning of Christmas." Most people know what Christmas is really about, so if that was going to be a turnoff for them, they could decide not to come.

We delivered invitations to forty-four houses. That's our whole street plus two cul-de-sacs. We made face-to-face contact with every single couple, most of whom we'd never met before. Then we did a lot of praying as we waited for RSVPs. Norm and Becky had a good feel for how many to invite and how many of those would come. Out of forty-four houses, fourteen couples showed up (this was a no-kids event). Including ourselves and our cohosts, there were thirty-two people altogether, which was just about right for the size of our house.

People mingled well because of the get-acquainted games we played. We ate lots of good food, sang Christmas carols, and shared holiday memories and traditions. There was not one unplanned minute. Even the music playing in the background had a strategy to it. ■

Bert:

Even though we hosted the party, we had a friend give the gospel presentation. That allowed us to be more relaxed. I also didn't want to have any "bait and switch" going on, where you say, "Come to a Christmas party," and then you hammer people with the gospel. My conscience was eased because of the wording on the invitation about sharing the true meaning of Christmas.

After all the neighbors shared their memories and traditions, one of our cohosts gave a brief testimony and spoke about Christmas. Then we passed out 3 x 5 cards and asked for comments about the party and future activities everyone might like to do. That ended the formal party, but it was still early and there was plenty of food left. We invited everyone to stay as long as they liked. Most stayed, but two or three couples immediately headed for the door.

Did it hurt when they made a beeline for the exit? Yeah, it did. But we still feel like we did the right thing. Anybody who's going to be involved in evangelism has to be prepared for a little awkwardness. While the talk of Christ might have been offensive to some, they now know we're Christians. They're going to be watching us. As they see how we live and how our kids act, our neighbors might say, "Hey, maybe there's something to that after all." Or if they're ever in a crisis, they may say, "Let's go talk to Bert and Lisa. Maybe they can help."

Even people who didn't come to the party were gratified to be invited. Some dropped by or sent us a Christmas note saying they were sorry they couldn't make it. Although they didn't attend the party, hand-delivering the invitations was a great way to meet them.

Before we moved, we prayed that we would be led to a neighborhood where we could be a positive influence. We don't feel like we're here by accident. That doesn't mean we weren't nervous about holding an evangelistic party or doing other outreach activities. But we left the results to the Lord. ■

DEFEATING FEAR

Bert and Lisa's experience represents what so many Christians could be doing in their neighborhoods. At their party, seven neighbors expressed interest in a discussion group about "life and God issues"—basically, a seeker's Bible study. Bert and Lisa have since developed strong friendships with several neighbors, including the one Lisa initially felt so burdened for.

Of course, fear will show itself the moment you even begin to think about hosting a neighborhood party. You'll immediately have a handful of excuses why it could never work. A word of encouragement: Everyone we have known who has hosted a neighborhood party has reported it to be a good and encouraging experience—every single one! Initially, most of the people who hosted parties had objections like these:

Hardly any of our neighbors would show up. We don't even know most of them. You will very likely be surprised. People long to meet their neighbors in a comfortable setting, and that's what you'll be providing. By hosting a party, you will give yourself a reason to knock on every door in your neighborhood. You will show your neighbors that you value them.

Our house is too small to invite the whole neighborhood in for a party. Then don't invite the *whole* neighborhood. Typically, only one-fourth to one-third of those you invite will attend. Just invite three to four times the number of people who could fit comfortably in your home.

It seems phony. I'd feel like I was setting a trap for my unsaved neighbors. Bert was absolutely right when he said people would feel manipulated if you pulled the old "bait and switch." It's important that a neighborhood party be about extending true friendship, not tricking your neighbors into hearing the gospel. God commands us to love our neighbors, and true love does not involve deceit or ulterior motives. If you plan to share the gospel at your party, the invitation needs to make reference to that.

Some of our neighbors are pretty scary people. I'm not sure I want them in my house. Think of it this way: Those scary neighbors need Jesus. God may have put you in your neighborhood to reach them. Is that worth a small risk? Also, if people show up at your party, they are at least a little open to your friendship. Who knows? They may become a lot less scary.

Several of our neighbors are Jewish (or Muslim, or Buddhist, or Mormon). It's okay to invite them as long as the party invitation tells them what to expect. For example, Bert and Lisa mentioned "the true meaning of Christmas" in their invitations. You may be surprised when people of other faiths come, if only to socialize and get to know the neighbors. What an opportunity to respectfully share Christ with people who need Him!

We are just not the party-hosting types. We're uncomfortable in that setting, even in someone else's home. We've all heard the phrase "step outside of your comfort zone" so much that it's become a cliché. But ask yourselves: What's more important, your comfort or your responsibility to love your neighbors? Be willing to stretch yourselves. God promises He'll be there with you. And your cohosts will help relieve your tension because you won't be in it alone.

We prefer to do things on a smaller scale, reaching out to one neighbor at a time rather than having a big, formal party. Those one-to-one relationships are vital, of course. But a party can change the tone of a whole neighborhood in one day. It may break down prejudices, fears, and isolation in a way that one-to-one relationships can't. You may be the catalyst for turning a lonely, cold neighborhood into a true community.

PLANNING YOUR PARTY

Now let's get down to the nitty-gritty. When you decide it's time to host a party, you'll want to plan each step carefully. Seemingly small details might be critically important. We'll assume here that you're planning a Christmas party, but the following steps can be adapted for any occasion:

Select the date

This is most important at Christmastime, when social calendars fill up. Make yours the first party your neighbors will attend. They'll compare the others to yours, and that's good. They'll remember the "light" they felt at your party. The first two weekends in December are the best time to beat the rush. Weeknights are okay, but weekends are better. Sunday nights are ideal because people tend to make fewer social plans then.

Decide who to invite

You've got several options when determining the guest list:

Adult couples (no kids). This is the most common scenario, with the whole neighborhood invited. Also consider inviting certain adults from your place of employment if there is room.

Ladies only. Often, the initial coming together as a neighborhood starts with the women and then spreads to the husbands and children. This could be a daytime gathering, but more likely it will be at night if many of the women in your neighborhood work outside the home.

Kids and parents. At Christmas, a "birthday party for Jesus" can be the hit of the neighborhood. Parties like this are effective at getting both children and parents together.

Recruit your cohosts

Prayerfully select mature believers from your church or neighborhood to be your behind-the-scenes support. Their names will be listed along with yours as the hosts on the invitations. Have a planning and prayer meeting at least once to review everything. At the party, cohosts take care of the food, drink refills, and other details, so the host couple can welcome and visit with their guests. Your cohosts will also be praying throughout the evening.

Prepare and deliver invitations

Invitations should give the basics: what, where, when (date and time), what to bring, what's on the agenda, and so forth. Ask for an RSVP at least two or three days before the party. You can make the invitations yourself by hand or on a computer, or order them from us at www.neighborhope.com. Here's one example:

Holidays are a special time for neighbors . . .
to make new friends . . . renew old friendships . . .
and enjoy one another's holiday traditions.
Please join us at

Our Neighborhood Christmas Party!
We will eat, visit, play games, laugh, sing old-time Christmas carols,
and share favorite Christmas memories.
Saturday, December 5
Jerry and Jeanne Ryan (#7 Maple Trail)
7 to 9:30 P.M.

Hosted by
Jerry and Jeanne Ryan, 555-8312
Dwight and Hilde Johnson, 555-9879
We will have a special time of sharing some inspirational thoughts
about the true meaning of Christmas.
RSVP by December 2. Adults only, please.
Please bring a favorite festive food to share. Beverages will be provided.

Personally delivering the invitations is the key to befriending every neighbor. Until now, you may not have had a valid reason to ring every doorbell on your block. Now you do! Even if some neighbors can't attend the party, you will have overcome the major barrier to friendship: not ever having met.

You don't need to prepare a long speech. For a Christmas party, just say something such as, "Hi, we're Norm and Becky Wretlind. We're your neighbors from down the street. We want to invite you to a neighborhood Christmas party on Saturday, December 5. It'll be a great time to get to know our neighbors. Here's an invitation with all the information. We'd love to have you come."

Deliver invitations about two weeks before the party. Go as a couple or take your kids along. If the people are not home, leave the invitation on or near the door so they're sure to see it. Then drop by a couple of days later to ask if they received it. Neighbors are sometimes hesitant to make new friends unless they truly feel wanted.

Recruit your prayer partners

Invite several believers to be your prayer partners for the event. Give them updates and prayer requests. Also, ask for prayers from your church, Sunday school class, and Bible study groups. God moves as His people pray—that's a promise!

Decide if babysitters are needed

This is no minor detail. Many parties have been sabotaged by the distractions of children entering the room and calling for their parents. The best option usually is to let the neighbors find their own babysitters. If that doesn't seem like it will work, you might provide someone from your church to care for the children at a nearby neighbor's home. The main issue is to control the environment at your party so your neighbors can experience its full benefits without distractions.

Plan food and beverages

Asking your neighbors to bring food makes this job much easier. More importantly, it gives everyone a sense of "ownership" of the party. Some hosts even ask guests to bring recipes to share.

As the hosts, you should provide all the beverages. This avoids having neighbors assume they should bring an alcoholic beverage. If they do, thank them for their kind gesture and simply place it alongside the other beverages. This really is a nonissue that Christians sometimes get too uptight about. The pace of your party won't allow alcohol to be a problem.

Plan to take photos or video the event

Your neighbors will enjoy seeing photos or a video of themselves at a later date. For instance, when a neighbor family moves away, a photo album comprised of pictures from neighborhood parties can make a nice going-away gift. Because you as the host couple will be preoccupied, it is best for one of your cohosts to be the designated photographer.

Plan to present parting gifts

This isn't absolutely necessary, but, especially at Christmastime, a meaningful gift that expresses the love of Christ can have a powerful effect.

Our website offers suggestions of gifts to give and where to get them. The following are just three of many ideas:

- Campus Crusade's *The JESUS Video*. Based on the gospel of Luke, this is one of the most historically accurate films ever made about the life of Christ. More than four billion people have now viewed it.

- *Why Christmas?* by Nicky Gumbel. This is a powerful booklet that communicates why Jesus is central to Christmas, why He came to live among us, why people need Him, and how they can respond to His offer of forgiveness and eternal life. It also speaks to many of the objections people have about Christ and provides evidence to support His claims.

- *The Christmas Sampler*. This booklet tells of the wonderful promise given to us in the Old Testament of a Savior who would come to redeem the world, shares the joyous fulfillment of that promise through His birth, and offers a challenge for readers to receive Him into their hearts.

Prepare a creative guest registration

Ask your guests to provide information that could be used to produce a neighborhood directory. (This can also serve as a prayer list for you.) A simple guest book works fine, or you can try something more creative. One idea is to draw a large map of your neighborhood with houses large enough for your guests to write their names (including children and pets), address, phone number, and e-mail address.

EXPECT A MIRACLE

When all the planning is finished, all that's left is to continue praying and then wait for your doorbell to ring on the night of the party. If you've never done this before (or even if you have!), you probably still won't feel totally prepared. That's normal. Realize, though, that each of these preparation steps is intended to bring Christ to your party.

Jesus loved a good party. The second chapter of John's gospel recounts the wedding at Cana, just up the road from Nazareth. Jesus and His disciples had been invited; in fact, the whole area probably had been. And Jesus chose this "neighborhood" celebration as the time to perform his first recorded miracle—turning water into wine (verses 1-11). We could debate the theological implications, but for the wedding guests, that miracle kept a good party going.

If you open your home to your neighbors, Jesus will show up, too. And He may just perform a miracle in their hearts.

CHAPTER SEVEN

IT'S PARTY TIME

"Follow me," Jesus said to him. . . . Then Levi held a great banquet for Jesus at his house, and a large crowd of tax collectors and others were eating with them.   LUKE 5:27,29

The invitations are delivered, your "halls are decked," and you've prayed daily for those who will attend your party. Finally, the big day arrives! Let's look at how the evening might go. We'll focus on a Christmas party, but again, these concepts can be adapted for any occasion.

There are a couple of approaches you can take, and both serve an eternal purpose.

Pre-evangelistic: This kind of party enables you and your neighbors to get better acquainted in a fun, nonthreatening way. You will also have opportunities to make it obvious that your relationship with Christ brings great joy and meaning to the celebration of Christmas. This will open doors for the future. If you don't know your neighbors well, or if you don't know where they stand on faith issues, this low-key approach is the logical way to start.

Evangelistic: A get-together with evangelism as its primary mission is, of course, more open and overt about sharing the gospel, but it is still done in a thoroughly appropriate and sensitive way. If you know your neighbors fairly well, you may sense the Lord saying, "This is the time to clearly communicate My message of salvation with your dear neighbors. Those who are responsive to your friendship are the ones I am drawing to myself." The invitation to your party should clearly state that you or a friend will share some "inspirational thoughts on the true meaning of Christmas." Then there will be no surprises for those who attend.

Whichever approach you choose, your party will likely follow a similar format and schedule. The event will probably last between two and three hours, plus mingling time as people prepare to leave.

ARRIVING AND MINGLING (30–45 MINUTES)

Be sure to have lively, contemporary holiday music playing and the tree lights lit as guests start arriving. You, or preferably one of your cohosts, should hang up their coats and take their food to the serving area. Then direct them to a table where they'll find name tags and the guest book. Have someone at the food table ready to serve punch or hot drinks. Warm hospitality is an important part of making your guests feel welcome. When the responsibilities are shared among several people, the mood is more relaxed and you as host are free to chat with people.

Here's one idea to get people talking: As your guests are filling out their name tags, have a cohost place "Who or What Am I?" stickers on their backs. A Christmas-related word or phrase, such as "Frosty the

Snowman" or "Figgy Pudding," is written on each sticker. Explain that they need to ask each of the other guests three "yes" or "no" questions about their sticker until they can guess what it says. When they guess correctly, they may place the sticker on their front. This game keeps everyone active as they are eating and waiting for others to arrive. (See Appendix A for more details.)

Guest Book

As we said in the last chapter, you will definitely want to have your neighbors sign a guest book when they arrive. This not only will give you a list of people to pray for, but it also will help network your neighborhood. You can ask them for their addresses and phone numbers, e-mail addresses, kids' names and ages, and even pets' names. Tell them that after the holidays, you will create a neighborhood directory and give a copy to everyone.

Four-Cornered Name Tags

These encourage people to share information they might not otherwise volunteer. Have guests write their names in the center and jot down their responses to the following in each of the four corners:

> Corner 1: Hometown
>
> Corner 2: Career/occupation
>
> Corner 3: Hobby
>
> Corner 4: Childhood hero

You can vary these themes if you wish. Just remember that the information shouldn't be anything too personal or uncomfortable to share. Later, each guest will explain his or her name tag as an introduction during the sharing time. Here's an example:

Hometown	Career/Occupation
YOUR NAME	
Hobby	Childhood Hero

PLAYING ICEBREAKER GAMES (20 MINUTES)

These games help people feel comfortable if played soon after all have arrived. We use games like Christmas Carol Quiz or Getting-to-Know-You Bingo. (See Appendix A for details.)

Hosts often are concerned that guests will feel silly or self-conscious playing party games. Not to worry! If the right games are selected—ones that don't put anyone on the spot and don't take a long time—the vast majority of people will participate enthusiastically. These games have been used for many years with both Christians and nonChristians and have proven to be a lot of fun.

SINGING CHRISTMAS CAROLS
(10–20 MINUTES)

This segment allows everyone to enjoy songs and prepares them to share holiday memories. Singing together can be a bonding time, creating a sense of unity and camaraderie. Be sure to sing secular as well as sacred songs. Let guests choose their favorites from a song sheet. A guitar or piano player would be a plus; maybe you could recruit one of the neighbors or someone from your church to play. Some groups even choose to go caroling together around the neighborhood. If you do this, you may want to skip the icebreaker game for the sake of time.

Using a set of hand-playable party chimes (available through NeighborHope at 800-873-8957) offers a unique variation to singing. Each guest is issued one chime and a clanger—a large nail, a metal spoon, or something similar. Each numbered chime plays a specific note on the chromatic scale. The songs' notes are converted to corresponding numbers that match the numbers of the chimes. Simply copy the sequence of numbers for each song you wish to play onto poster board so all players will be able to see. The host directs the songs by touching the numbers with a pointer in the correct rhythm. Melodies are created as guests follow the chart and strike their own chime at just the right moment (similar to a bell choir). This requires concentration and teamwork and results in a lot of laughter. The set comes with a songbook containing popular Christmas carols as well as other traditional songs for year-round family entertainment. These chimes have been a true favorite for group participation any time of the year.

Sharing Christmas Memories and Traditions (30–40 Minutes)

This will be the evening's highlight, and you will learn more about your neighbors than you ever imagined. The host usually serves as moderator. Avoid interruptions by placing cohosts near the entry door to greet late-comers and near the phone to catch incoming calls.

We suggest you open the time by calling everyone together in one room and saying something such as, "One of our favorite aspects of Christmas is recalling memorable events and traditions from our child-hoods. I'll bet we all have more in common than we realize. Let's see if I'm right as we share some memories about Christmas with one another. I'd like us to take turns sharing briefly on either of these questions: What is one of your favorite childhood Christmas memories or traditions? or What is the true meaning of Christmas to you? Start by telling us your name and the answers from the four corners of your name tag. To give you all time to collect your thoughts, I've asked my wife to go first."

As hosts, you will set the tone for the level of sharing desired. Strive to be somewhat vulnerable, humorous, interesting, and nostalgic. A spouse or a cohost should begin with something on the lighter side. It might sound something like this:

My most treasured memory has to do with a family tradition I looked forward to each December. My entire extended family would go downtown to visit a bank that had been transformed into a winter wonderland. The highlight of that time, though, was the gingerbread and wassail they served. We would gather

together with those refreshments and catch up with one
another about the events in our lives over the previous few
months. Once we'd eaten our fill, we would head across the
street to another bank that had assembled a huge choir.
Although none of us could carry a tune in a bucket, it didn't
matter as we belted out those songs we had sung for years and
knew by heart.

Do *not* begin with a spiritual memory. It may make some people uncomfortable, thinking they are expected to talk about something spiritual as well. At the end, after all the neighbors have had a chance to talk, the host/moderator can share the true meaning of Christmas.

If a guest or two are particularly long-winded, simply interject a comment here and there to keep things moving from person to person. You will find that neighbors have wanted to have a conversation like this but have not been given the opportunity. Many will thank you afterward.

SHARING THE TRUE MEANING OF CHRISTMAS (15 MINUTES)

There are endless ways to talk about the essence of the gospel. Prayerfully seek God's direction for your party. He will enable you to be bold about your faith as well as sensitive to the proper way to communicate it.

As the moderator, the way you begin should flow naturally out of the memory-sharing that has just preceded you. That doesn't mean, however, that you can't practice beforehand with your spouse or a friend until you become comfortable with what you might say. You may want to begin with one of your fondest Christmas traditions or joke about the most unusual gift you ever received before launching into the heart of your message.

At a pre-evangelistic party: If, during the memory-sharing time, you talked about a funny gift you've received, you then can talk about Christ as the greatest gift you've ever received. When you talk about the real meaning of Christmas, weave in how knowing Jesus Christ personally has made Christmas—and your entire life—more meaningful. Because all the guests were given the freedom to share what they wanted to, you certainly can do the same with confidence. But don't preach! Simply speak from your heart, telling about your own experience. (Words like, "Repent, ye generation of sinners!" will send guests running for the door.) And avoid Christian clichés that are meaningful to you but would sound awfully foreign to those outside the faith ("I was redeemed, washed in the blood, sanctified, saved. . . .").

If you have trouble coming up with a personal story, a well-chosen Christmas reading can work. That allows you to include something more specific about the true meaning of Christmas by sharing someone else's words. There are many good readings to choose from. Examine some of the Christmas tracts at a bookstore or excerpts in Christian magazines or websites. Or you can simply read the Christmas story (Luke 2:1-20) from the *New Living Translation* or *The Message*.

At a pre-evangelistic party: The goal is to share the true meaning of Christmas in such a way that your neighbors will know that you sincerely believe in Christ and that you are approachable about the subject. What you say will not only let your neighbors know what you believe, but it will also open doors for future conversations about how they, too, can have a relationship with Christ.

At an evangelistic party: After the group sharing time, you and/or your spouse (or an invited guest speaker) can *briefly* give your testimony with the gospel clearly explained. Again, with either type of party, no surprises: Be sure the invitation has stated openly that someone will share inspirational thoughts about the true meaning of Christmas. Here's an example of what might be shared:

I remember one year in particular. I was home from college and was really looking forward to seeing friends and family. As usual, we headed over to the bank downtown, ate more gingerbread than we needed to, and then proceeded to the next bank for a sing-along. But this year something was different. When we began to sing the Christmas carols, they took on a whole new meaning to me. The songs that I once had sung by heart, I now was singing *with* my heart.

I remember singing, "Joy to the world, the Lord has come! Let earth receive her King; Let every heart prepare him room." As I sang those words, a true sense of joy overwhelmed me. I realized for the first time what they really meant. You see, just a few months earlier, a friend had explained to me the true meaning of Christmas. He told how the greatest gift ever given was Jesus Christ, who came to earth as a baby but went on to die on the cross to pay the penalty for all the wrong things I had done. I then realized I could do what the song encourages: I could prepare room in my heart for Him and invite Him into my life to forgive me of my sins and bring me into a relationship with God.

That day, Christmas took on a whole new meaning because it reminded me that the Son of God not only came into the world by being born in a manger on that first Christmas, but also came into my life to restore my relationship with God and give me joy, not just on Christmas, but every day of my life.

You might feel nervous sharing so openly, but this is an awesome privilege. Nonbelievers rarely hear from a husband and wife about how Jesus changes lives. We suggest you end your talk by saying something like, "If any of you would like to hear more about how our faith in Christ has changed our lives, we would love to talk with you." If you feel it's appropriate and you sense people are particularly open to what you've said, you might include an opportunity for people to pray to receive Christ. This may be the night some of your neighbors open their hearts to the Lord!

If you don't feel comfortable giving this talk—especially if it would keep you from having a party at all—by all means invite your cohosts or another Christian couple who communicates well to share their testimonies. Don't let this be a make-it-or-break-it issue for you. In fact, it's sometimes more effective if the person sharing the gospel is not the host. That way, the host can be just a "normal" neighbor extending love and kindness—and opening doors for deeper discussions later on.

Because this part of the evening is central to your purpose for giving the party, let us go into more detail about how to make your talk effective.

Transition

A personal testimony provides a natural introduction to sharing the gospel. Having told your neighbors how the message of Christ has changed your life, you can then discuss the content of that message and how you responded to God's offer of forgiveness and eternal life. Example: "A friend explained to me the true meaning of Christmas. He then talked about four very important truths from the Bible that have radically changed my life. I'd like to share them with you briefly."

Explaining the gospel

Presenting the gospel involves explaining its four main truths. As you share each, try to relate it to the meaning of Christmas. Several outlines are available in booklets such as *Would You Like to Know God Personally?* (Campus Crusade for Christ), *The Bridge to Life* (The Navigators), and *Steps to Peace with God* (Billy Graham Association). These and other resources can be found at Christian bookstores or online. You may also want to memorize Scripture verses to reinforce the significance of each point. Avoid reading the information to your guests. Rather, adapt these resources to the context of a Christmas party and share them as your own thoughts flow naturally.

The four main truths of the gospel are as follows (adapted from *Would You Like to Know God Personally?*):

1. God loves you and created you to know Him personally.
2. People are sinful and separated from God, so we cannot know Him personally or experience His love on our own.
3. Jesus Christ is God's only provision for our sin. Through Him alone we can know God personally and experience His love.
4. We must individually receive Jesus Christ as Savior and Lord; then we can know God personally and experience His love.

To illustrate the fourth point, you might say, "At Christmastime, people love to give gifts to one another, but the gifts we are given only truly become ours when we accept them from the giver. Likewise, God's greatest gift to us, the gift of forgiveness and eternal life, is ours only when we accept it by inviting Jesus Christ to come into our lives."

Concluding prayer

As you close the evening, it will be important to give your neighbors an opportunity to respond to what you've shared. You certainly don't want to cram the gospel down people's throats, and you don't want to *close* doors rather than open them. But remember, this may be the only time someone has personally invited them to receive Christ. Therefore, we think it's worth the risk if you sense even a little bit of receptivity from your guests. Here's an example of what you might say:

> I'd like to take a moment to thank God for the fun we've had together tonight and to pray for our neighborhood and our

nation. I also want to give you the opportunity to receive God's greatest gift to us: His Son, Jesus Christ. Remember the carol, "Joy to the world, the Lord has come! Let earth receive her King; Let every heart prepare him room." As I close our time with a prayer, if you would like to prepare room in your heart for Christ and invite Him into your life to forgive your sins and give you eternal life, just pray silently as I pray out loud.

Dear heavenly Father, I want to thank you for all these wonderful friends and the fun we have shared tonight. I pray for all of us neighbors in this coming year, that you would bless us with good health, stable jobs, and unified families. We also ask your favor on our president and our nation's leaders. As Christmas approaches, help us to remember the gift of your Son, who you sent to bring joy to the world and forgiveness and eternal life to those who would accept Him. Father, I pray that if there is anyone here tonight who has never accepted the gift of your Son, that they would pray this prayer with me: "Dear Jesus, thank you for the incredible gift of forgiveness and eternal life that you offer me because you died on the cross for my sins. Right now, I accept that gift and open the door of my life to receive you as my Savior and Lord. Please come into my life to forgive me of my sins, to give me eternal life, and to begin making me into the person you created me to be. Amen."

INVITING RESPONSE AND PLANNING THE NEXT EVENT (15 MINUTES)

Whether your party is pre-evangelistic or evangelistic, a primary purpose is to generate warmth and begin ongoing relationships. You can take that next step by offering a simple get-together in the middle of January when you might have the neighborhood directory available. For instance, you could plan a "cabin fever" gathering to play table games, have coffee, and talk. Maybe the kids can be invited this time. The people who come to that gathering definitely are expressing a desire for deeper friendships.

At a pre-evangelistic party: Hand out blank 3 x 5 cards and pencils. Say something like, "This has been a great evening. We are so glad each of you came. Please do us a favor and jot down some comments about the evening. Put your name at the top. I'll give you a few minutes to write."

As they are finishing, say, "I'm sure all of us have other great ideas for activities we as neighbors can do together throughout the year. On the back of your card, please jot down a couple of ideas. We'll share them soon with everyone."

At an evangelistic party: At the end of the talk, the speaker hands out 3 x 5 cards and pencils and asks for guests' names and comments on the evening, especially the inspirational talk. He or she invites them to put an X on the card if they prayed to receive Christ. It's important to give your neighbors a specific opportunity to acknowledge their response to the gospel. Next, the speaker offers to send new believers a follow-up booklet such as *Beginning with Christ* (NavPress). Finally, the speaker or host asks them to jot down ideas for future neighborhood gatherings on the backs of the cards.

If you want to start a neighborhood Bible study within a month or two, you as the host should mention the idea as people are writing. Because they are offering their ideas, it's certainly proper for you to offer yours. Say something like,

> One desire we've had is to have a four- to six-week open discussion about life and God issues and what the Bible says about those things. Maybe you've never read the Bible, but if you would like to discover for yourself what it says and would like to get to know some of the neighbors even more, then please join us. You don't need to have your own Bible. We'll have extra ones available. Just write the word *discussion* in the right-hand corner of your card. We'll call you to figure out a day and time.

If you have selected a Bible study booklet, you might show it at this time.

Have everyone fold their cards, and then pass a basket to collect them (this is best) or have your guests leave them in a certain spot. Thank them again for coming. Invite them to stay to enjoy more food and conversation. Be especially alert about anyone who seems to have warmed up to your friendship. This could be someone God is drawing to Himself through you!

As your party wraps up, you can give your guests a parting gift with a spiritual message, as mentioned in chapter 6. This token of friendship will nourish the seeds you've planted.

AFTER THE PARTY

Immediately after the party concludes, get together with your Christian cohosts and other support couples to read the response cards. You will be thrilled and blessed! Thank God for all He has done, rejoice together, and pray for future opportunities. Then clean up and enjoy a well-earned night of rest.

The next week, do the following:

1. Fill out "Your After-Party Questionnaire." (See Appendix C.) You may want to give a copy to your pastor or your church's evangelism coordinator. Also, ask to share about your experience in your Sunday school class, worship service, or Bible study group.

2. Thank all of your prayer partners and give them a report. Call others in your church who may be holding similar parties to encourage them and pass along ideas.

3. Jot down desires and ideas the Holy Spirit is giving you for the coming year. (See the planning suggestions in Appendix D.)

4. Create the neighborhood directory and plan to deliver it within the next month. This will give you another intentional contact with your neighbors. Also, visit with each one who indicated an interest in a Bible study.

5. Make a new prayer list of your neighbors and continue to water the seeds that have been planted by having family prayer times and taking prayer walks in your neighborhood.

6. Arrange to get together after the holidays with your pastor and others who had parties to pray, talk about your experiences, and discuss future plans. Consider training other church members and even people in other churches.

OTHER TYPES OF PARTIES

Almost all of the ideas we've given you for a neighborhood Christmas party can be adapted for parties at other times of the year. The keys will always be the four-cornered name tags, the icebreaker games, the time of sharing, and the transition into talking about Christ. A few examples of topics for group sharing and their natural transitions are as follows:

- Independence Day: Ask your guests to tell what America means to them, and bring the conversation around to what it means to be truly free in Christ.

- Valentine's Day: Invite your guests to share a favorite memory of their wedding or honeymoon, and then transition into Jesus' ultimate example of love.

- Easter: Each guest shares a favorite Easter memory and talks about what the true meaning of Easter is. Then explain how the resurrection of Jesus is what gives us true hope.

- Labor Day: This holiday usually marks the end of summer and the beginning of a new school year. It's a great opportunity for a neighborhood picnic or barbecue. Parents can talk about school memories (favorite teachers, athletic achievements, and so on), and kids can mention what they're looking forward to during the coming year. Then transition into discussing new beginnings and fresh starts—the kind Christ provides when we become new creatures in Him.

With a little creative planning on your part, any holiday or celebration can open the door to neighborhood hospitality and allow you to share the message of Christ in a nonthreatening and fun way.

CONCLUDING THOUGHTS

Perhaps the greatest fear for those considering hosting a party is this: *What if we alienate a neighbor by talking about Christ? How do we go about patching things up?*

At a party we hosted several years ago, one of our neighbors shared on his 3 x 5 card his disdain that we had made it a religious event. That may happen, no matter how tactful you are or how much notice you give on the invitation. Call or stop by the person's house a day or two later to express concern that he or she was offended. You don't need to apologize for making God a part of your Christmas party, but you can genuinely say you're sorry that aspects of the event caused the individual discomfort. Showing grace and humility at a decisive moment like this can open doors as well. Be willing to engage in further conversation if he or she is open to it.

Another common concern is, *What if someone asks me a question about Christianity that I don't know the answer to?* Simply say, "That's a great question. I need to find the answer to that myself. Let me do some research and get back to you. Could we get together next week?" If the person is sincerely interested, he or she will accept your invitation.

Through it all, cut yourself lots of slack and give yourself room for imperfection. God will surely bless your efforts and your love for your neighbors. You may never know this side of heaven how your kindness has influenced those around you. Then again, you may!

CHAPTER EIGHT

CREATING A NEIGHBORHOOD FELLOWSHIP

Every day they continued to meet together in the temple courts. They broke bread in their homes and ate together with glad and sincere hearts, praising God and enjoying the favor of all the people. And the Lord added to their number daily those who were being saved.   ACTS 2:46-47

A party is often the first big step toward connecting a neighborhood. In what might have been a closed and unfriendly place, suddenly neighbors will begin smiling and waving at each other . . . honking the car horn as they drive past . . . walking across the street to say hello to someone working in the yard.

In short, your party will make a difference. Sometimes, especially if your party is well attended, that change may be immediate and obvious. Sometimes it won't be. If turnout is low, positive response sparse, or the spiritual portion a little flat, it may be a while before you see the effects.

Our longtime friends Dwight and Hilde Johnson know that uneasy feeling. They came to Christ during our years together in Richardson—a story you'll read about later in this chapter. More recently, they've impacted their neighborhood in Garland, Texas.

Hilde:

We've been living in our current neighborhood for about thirteen years. Three years ago, I felt God leading me to have a Christmas party. So we hosted one. I talked about what Christmas means to me as a Christian. I kept it very nonthreatening because we really didn't know our neighbors very well.

Nothing happened after that. I was disappointed, but I knew God was in control so I was at peace about it. Then the following December, one of our nonChristian neighbors decided he wanted to host that year's party because he'd had so much fun at ours. He did, and a couple came who hadn't attended the year before. I started talking to them at the party and found out that the woman's husband was a Christian, but she wasn't.

This woman and I were drawn to each other, and I kept in contact with her. She started coming to a ladies' Bible study with me at our church. A couple weeks later, I felt led to share the gospel with her, and she prayed to receive Christ. Today, her whole family is part of our church.

God had a plan. Our party wasn't for nothing. If we hadn't had it, then our neighbor wouldn't have had a party the next year, and that new couple wouldn't have come. You just never know what will happen. God uses anything, even when from our point of view it seems like a failure. ∎

THE NEXT STEP: A NEIGHBORHOOD BIBLE STUDY

Whatever the immediate results of your party, your obedience will spark something. With God's help, you will create a "spiritual snowball" and set it in motion from the top of a hill. How far it rolls and how large it grows is up to God and your willingness to keep obeying Him.

So what's next? After a Christmas party, a less formal follow-up event like a family game night or Super Bowl party can continue building friendships. If any of your guests expressed interest in a neighborhood Bible study, contact them within the next week or two and set a date for an informational meeting.

As the book of Acts tells us, new believers and seekers share a common interest and will want to meet together. We have found this often begins with a women's Bible study group. We certainly don't mean to rule out forming a men's group right away—it's just not the most common scenario. Even today, with many women working full-time, women tend to be more sensitive to family and relational issues than men are.

Whether it begins with women, men, or couples, a neighborhood Bible study will become a welcoming, spiritual hub for your neighborhood. For starters, try following these steps:

1. As we said in the last chapter, announce the study at your initial party and invite your guests to indicate their interest on their comment cards. Don't necessarily call it a *study*, though. How attractive does that sound to an already busy person? Besides, a group of seekers may have little idea what a Bible study really is. Instead, we call it "a discussion group on life and God issues."

2. Pray faithfully for your neighbors by name. Ask God to work in their lives and to create a hunger to know Him. Consider taking prayer walks through your neighborhood.

3. Gather a team of people committed to working together, using their gifts to facilitate an evangelistic, small-group study. One person can handle hospitality. He or she will host the gathering, greet each member, and coordinate food. Another can teach the group. This person will determine the type of study most appropriate for your neighbors, prepare lessons, and provide study guides and other resource materials. It is not necessary to have a team, but it may prove helpful. If you do decide to form one, choose Christians in your neighborhood, if at all possible. Involve them in the process from the beginning, so they can build relationships with your neighbors, too.

4. Assess the needs of the group, either before or during the first meeting. Prayerfully determine what most fits your neighbors' interests: seeking answers to apologetic questions; studying the life of Christ; studying the Bible to understand what it says and how it relates to them; or studying a particular topic or issue, such as marriage enrichment, parenting, or finances.

5. Choose the curriculum your group will study based on your evaluation of their needs. Your church or Christian bookstore will have a long list of available materials.

6. Conduct a four- to eight-week session. Make sure everyone knows up front what they are committing to and what is expected of them (attendance and preparation). After the initial time period, ask if they'd like to continue meeting together. You may want to add other neighbors at that time who were not able to attend at first.

7. Continue to build your relationships with the group outside of study time. Ask God to give you other opportunities to discuss what's been covered in the study. Plan social activities for the group, too.

A successful neighborhood Bible study, even if it's small, builds spiritual unity. As neighbors get to know each other better, more spiritual conversations will take place. A Bible study is a natural environment to invite neighbors to continue those conversations. In our Texas neighborhood, it became the catalyst for a true neighborhood fellowship.

GOD TRANSFORMS A NEIGHBORHOOD

We moved to Richardson, Texas, in August 1973, desiring for God to use us to reach our new neighborhood. Not in our wildest dreams would we have imagined what would happen there during the following three years.

Our subdivision was fairly new and attractive to professionals— many of them salespeople—who had been transferred to Dallas from all over the country. A clubhouse, a swimming pool, and tennis courts were available to everyone who lived there.

The neighborhood was made up primarily of young couples with families. There were kids everywhere, mostly elementary-school age or younger. That gave the parents a lot of common ground. Frequent adult parties were already going on—many at the clubhouse and most involving lots of alcohol. People were new to the area and looking for friendships. A few couples were native Texans, such as Patrick and Barbara McGee, but they were the exceptions. And we'd soon find out that people from every imaginable church background lived in the neighborhood. On the other hand, some obviously hadn't set foot in a church in many years.

About a month after we moved in, our next-door neighbors, who had brought over Texas iced tea the day we moved in, helped us organize a Sunday afternoon open house in our new home. Twenty-eight people came. We were overjoyed with the chance to establish friendships so quickly, and we had a sense that God was up to something.

As people came in the door that day, we asked them to sign our guest book. Afterward, we kept that book on our kitchen table. Once a day, as we held hands with our daughters around our meal, we prayed for all those neighbors, asking God to work in their lives and to continue to form friendships. Above all, we prayed that they would be saved.

During the next three years, we helped neighbors host Christmas parties, a women's Valentine's Day coffee, a couples' pool party, a kids' backyard Bible club, a weekend marriage seminar in the neighborhood clubhouse, and three weekly Bible studies (one for women, one for men, and one for couples). By God's work and to His glory alone, we saw more than sixty neighbors come to know Christ, including nine of the twenty-eight who had attended that first open house.

Maybe the best way to illustrate this "God happening" is through the eyes of a few of the couples whose lives were changed. As you read, think of that spiritual snowball rolling downhill.

Dennis Simonetta:

The first time I met Norm, he and his family had just moved in. We were living on two different streets connected by an alley. We happened to be out emptying trash at the same time one afternoon. He introduced himself and made some small talk. Then he started asking if we went to church and mentioned something about God. I stopped him and told him we were okay with our religion and didn't need to hear any of that. If he wanted to be a good neighbor, I said, we could get along without that kind of conversation. He said fine, no problem. And we said goodbye. ■

Sharon Simonetta:

Dennis and I both met Norm and Becky a week or two later at their open house. It was different from the get-togethers we were used to because there was no alcohol. But it was a nice opportunity to meet them and talk to everybody in the neighborhood. Then, three months later, they invited us to a Christmas party for our two streets. ■

Dennis:

It was going to be a traditional Christmas party, including singing Christmas carols. It sounded like fun. The invitation said that a couple would share what the meaning of Christmas was to them. That didn't sound offensive to me.

We went and had fun caroling and talking. Then we listened to a couple share their testimony along with a Christmas message. It all just made sense to me. We'd been searching for answers and trying various churches at that time, and my heart was ready. I put my faith in Christ that night. Sharon made her decision that night, too.

After we received Christ, we got excited and started telling others in the neighborhood about what we were experiencing. One of the guys, Dwight Johnson, happened to work with me. He and his wife, Hilde, went bowling every Sunday night with the two of us. We started sharing Christ with them, but they didn't seem too comfortable with that. ■

Hilde:

Sharon kept inviting me to a neighborhood Bible study that had begun as a result of the Christmas party. I told her no two or three times, and then I started feeling bad about it. I asked my husband, "Do you think I should go?" He said, "Well, you've always wanted to know more about God. Maybe this is your chance to find out."

So I went. For the first time, I found out that there was actually something written that came from God and that God was real. At first, when Becky asked me if I wanted to accept Christ, I said, "No, I've got to do some housecleaning first. I can't ask God to come into my life yet." But she explained to me that I couldn't do that housecleaning; Jesus had to do that. And that's when I accepted Christ. It was really exciting for me to find out that God loves me and to have a hope I hadn't had before. That excitement was a little overwhelming for my husband. ■

Dwight:

I thought she'd flipped out. I'd heard about people turning to Christ, but I always thought religion was a crutch for those who couldn't make it on their own. Now I had one of them living with me! Over the years, I'd heard Billy Graham and people like that speak. But we were Catholics, and that was good enough for me. We went to Mass probably 90 percent of the time. I'd put in my forty-five minutes a week, and that, too, was enough. At the time, I felt our life was really good. We had a nice home, a nice neighborhood, good kids, a good job. There wasn't anything I could see that we needed.

Hilde and some of the other women from the Bible study had been planning a neighborhood pool party at the Simonettas'. I didn't really want to go because Hilde had told me that some guests were planning to talk about their experience with God. But finally I said, "Well, I guess it won't hurt me to hear these people."

There were thirty or forty people there that night. The couple they had selected to share their testimony, Bob and Amy George, were very much like us. Bob was working part-time in ministry, but he had been a successful salesman. Amy, like Hilde, was from Germany. We both had young families. When Bob shared the gospel at that party, it made a lot of sense to me. I realized I had kind of locked God out of my life for many, many years. I accepted Christ that night. ■

Hilde:

We kept having different parties and gatherings, many of them at the clubhouse. Quite a few neighbors came to know the Lord through them. It was incredible. ■

Sharon:

The following December, our neighborhood Christmas party was at the clubhouse, and the Johnsons, Dennis, and I all shared our testimonies in front of almost a hundred neighbors. We were scared to death, but we got through it, and it went well. ■

Jeanne Ryan:

My husband, Jerry, and I were one of the couples invited to that neighborhood Christmas party. I wanted to go, but Jerry didn't. I said to him, "Look at all the work these people have done to put this thing together. We should at least show up."

After hearing the Simonettas and the Johnsons share their testimonies at the party, my impression was, *If God really is important in my life, I should be able to share something like that, too.* Jerry and I had both attended church and had gone to parochial schools. We were churched out. But I had no idea what a personal relationship with God could mean in my life.

After that party, I decided to start going to the neighborhood Bible study. In the meantime, I met Hilde, who was a back-door neighbor of ours. She would start sentences with, "Since I've become a Christian . . ." That puzzled me, because I figured if you were born in America and you weren't Jewish, you were Christian.

I could feel a lot going on in my head over those few months. I questioned who I was, where I was, and where I was going. I felt as if I was missing something but didn't know how to get it. One day after Bible study, Becky asked me if I knew how to tell someone else how to become a Christian. I began searching in my mind. A few days later, I reread the *Four Spiritual Laws* booklet that Becky had given me. I got to the part about 1 John 5:13, which says you can know that you have eternal life. And I thought, *Well, how can I know for sure?* I read the booklet again with that in mind, and all of a sudden everything made sense. The puzzle came together. I prayed to accept Christ.

Nobody had pressured me. It was all from within and triggered by little things people said—just normal conversation when they were talking about their relationship with Christ. ■

Jerry Ryan:

After that Christmas party, we did grow closer to many of the people there, but I felt that they were just nice folks. What they were doing was fine; it just wasn't for me. After a while, Jeanne and our six kids started attending Fellowship Bible Church. I didn't mind that, either. In fact, I liked having Sunday morning to myself to read the paper.

But as time went on, I could see that she and the kids were actually *enjoying* church. Occasionally I went with them, and we made a lot more friends. I began attending fairly regularly, and I heard the message about salvation every week. But I still didn't grasp it. Finally, on a Sunday morning in January 1976, a speaker during the service laid it out clearly for me. I accepted Christ that day.

During those months leading up to that Sunday, I *felt* the warmth before I *saw* the light. The warmth came from the people we were meeting and from that Christmas party. Some had been Christians for a long time. Most, however, were new believers. ■

Jeanne:

These people reached out to us at a significant time in our lives. We had small children, and we craved fellowship. We saw something in these people that we had never seen before. We started having Bible studies in our home in 1975—even before Jerry was a believer. He was very sarcastic about my "new religion." But Norm and Becky were always there, saying, "God's working on him. Don't worry." ■

Dwight:

So Norm and Becky reached the Simonettas, who reached us. And then we reached the Ryans, who reached another family. . . . And on it went. It wasn't dependent upon one couple. It was a neighborhood fellowship that so many people played a part in. ■

Sharon:

It did start, though, with Norm and Becky—their obedience to the Lord and their involvement in everything. Their home was open to everybody. It was the way God used them. He had that neighborhood earmarked for some reason. ■

Jeanne:

A neighbor of ours was a very bold New Yorker, so I was comfortable being bold with her, too, in talking about Christ. She ended up dying of cancer a few years later, but not before she had accepted Christ, moved to Little Rock, and led oncologists, neighbors, and others to the Lord. You just never know how God will work. When we get to heaven and hear some of the stories that we could never know in this life, we'll be amazed. ■

Becky:

One activity or group led to another. Everything happened so fast that we could barely keep up with all the people coming to Christ. At first, the ladies' Bible study became the hub for the spiritual interest that was growing among both believers and seekers. To kick off the study, we decided to hold a Valentine's Day evangelistic coffee for women. That morning, four women responded to our speaker's invitation to accept Christ.

That number soon increased to five. Mary Pat Parma talked to me for a few minutes after the coffee. She seemed very interested in what the speaker had said about her own relationship with God. I encouraged her to go home and read the book of John to learn more about Jesus. She did, and she read Romans, too. Three days later, I heard a knock at my front door. There was Mary Pat with her big St. Bernard, Bruno. Tears began to flow as she told me she'd prayed to accept Christ in her bathroom the day before. I began to cry, too. We hugged and cried together, rejoicing over what God had done. She said, "This is for real. Jesus is for real. I know He is."

In the coming weeks, Mary Pat was still a little skeptical of our neighborhood women's Bible study. After all, she reasoned, shouldn't Bible knowledge come from an expert, rather than just a group of neighbors talking and praying? She enrolled in a university Bible course, but that turned out to be an attack on her new faith, rather than an encouragement of it. She finally decided to give the Bible study a try.

"I'm realizing," she told me, "that I can read the Bible on my own. I don't have to go to an academic authority to tell me what it says."

Others realized the same thing. The women's study eventually grew so large that it branched into three groups. Mary Pat became the teaching leader of one of these groups. She had a women's coffee in her new neighborhood adjacent to ours, and three ladies accepted Christ. (By the way, Mary Pat has been teaching neighborhood women's Bible studies ever since.) The women's studies eventually led to a neighborhood men's group on Saturday mornings, then a couples' group one evening a week.

It's important to note that after the initial open house and the Christmas party, none of this group activity took place in our house on a regular basis. It was spread around to many different homes. We wanted our neighbors to feel that this was a "neighborhood happening," not just something Norm and I were spearheading. ■

Forming a Church

Our church, Fellowship Bible Church, played a vital role in all of this, too. While some neighbors chose to stay in their original churches, many others asked where we attended and started coming with us. Ours was a vibrant, contemporary church seven miles away in Dallas, pastored by Dr. Gene A. Getz, who, not so incidentally, placed a big emphasis on church planting. The church was bursting at the seams with new attenders, due in no small part to what was going on in Richardson. One Sunday morning as we drove down Arapahoe Road toward church, we counted forty-nine neighbors driving with us.

We often shared Communion during Bible studies. On one such occasion in the McGees' home, Dennis Simonetta remarked, "You know, we do the same thing at Fellowship Bible Church. Why don't *we* become a church?" And before long, we did just that. In September 1976, exactly three years after our first open house for the neighborhood, Richland Bible Fellowship Church was born in Richardson, Texas.

We began looking for a new church home right in our neighborhood and settled on Yale Elementary School. On our first Sunday, more than two hundred people attended, and we continued to grow from there. Every Sunday morning for the next three years, we transformed the school cafeteria into a sanctuary and classrooms for the kids. The Ryans kept all of the chairs and equipment in a trailer behind their house. On Sundays when no one could be found with a trailer hitch, several of the men would drag the trailer to the school.

Finally, a permanent home became available: the very clubhouse and pool area where so many neighborhood parties had taken place. The developer of our subdivision had gone bankrupt, and the church was able to purchase the facility for an attractive price. Our church grew quickly, drawing not only from our neighborhood, but also from surrounding neighborhoods.

Today, a three-story sanctuary and huge classroom buildings fill the property. The three tennis courts became a parking lot. The swimming pool continues to be a neighborhood gathering spot during the warm months—not only for swimming, but also for baptisms. Richland Bible Fellowship Church draws about 1,300 "neighbors" every Sunday, all because a few people decided to obey God and truly love their neighbors.

WHY IT ALL HAPPENED

Most often, God does extraordinary work through very ordinary people. Those of us in that neighborhood look back at those glorious years in Texas and wonder: *Why did God choose that neighborhood? How did other Christian couples, who never before had been able to reach out to neighbors, come out of their shells? How did so many people come to Christ in such a short time?*

Barbara McGee:

We have analyzed that over and over through the years. I don't know the answer, other than the Lord wanted it to happen right there, right then. Before Patrick and I moved to Richardson from Austin, and before Norm and Becky came from Anaheim, we were all praying that the Lord would put us in the neighborhood where He wanted us. And He answered those prayers. The Lord moved in miraculous ways in the lives of so many people. ■

Patrick McGee:

We had always been leaders in a church. But before we moved to Richardson, we'd grown dissatisfied. There was nothing particularly wrong; I had just begun to think that there had to be more to the Christian life than what we were experiencing. I had thought a lot about Galatians 2:20: "I have been crucified with Christ and I no longer live, but Christ lives in me." That verse spoke to me and turned my life around. It showed me that there was an abundant life waiting. God started working in our lives in a much greater way because we were letting Him do that. ■

Hilde:

I think it had a lot to do with the fact that so many adults were becoming Christians. When you become a Christian as an adult and you realize fully God's grace and the ways He changes your heart, that's really exciting. It's very different from having grown up with that because it's such a change in your life. And because you're so excited about what you found, you want to tell others. ■

MOVING ON

In 1989, after almost seventeen amazing years in Texas, we moved once again to be near Norm's family in Denver. Leaving that church and those dear friends was incredibly difficult. They gave us an overwhelming farewell with countless hugs, tears, and expressions of gratitude. Though we hated to leave, we knew the church was strong and in good hands. King Nash, one of our neighbors who came to Christ, commented, "It's comparable to the evangelism of Paul, who would establish a church and form a solid foundation. Then he would leave, and everything would keep on running. He kept tabs on their progress, but he didn't have to be there to lead anymore."

There are so many amazing stories from Richardson that they easily could fill another book. Many of our close friends from that neighborhood no longer live there, and they're quick to say they have never lived in another neighborhood quite like it. Frankly, neither have we. And maybe that's God's way of telling us—and you—that He uses different people in different ways at different times, all for His glory. Wherever your neighborhood and whatever your circumstances, He is ready to use you to draw people to Himself.

CHAPTER NINE

Reality Check: Handling

Tough Situations

Some people are content to remain within the shadow of the church. But as for me, give me a rescue station one yard from the gates of hell itself.

C. T. STUDD, EVANGELIST

We once lived next door to a couple who fought all the time. At night sometimes, we'd be lying in bed with the windows closed, and we'd still hear them screaming at each other inside their house. When that happened, we would get on our knees and pray that they wouldn't hurt or kill each other. We knew them a little; they knew us enough to know we were Christians.

Becky:

Once I invited the woman, who I'll call Stacey, to our neighborhood Bible study. But she said she wasn't interested in anything like that. She had a career and was a "weekend mom."

One night during an awful fight, Stacey finally called the police on her husband. She told him, loudly enough for the neighborhood to hear, that she wanted a divorce.

The next morning, her husband, Al, knocked on our door. Norm was at work, but my mother and aunt happened to be visiting, so I felt safe inviting him in. Al was a totally broken man and didn't know what to do. For some reason, he felt free to come to our house. I sat him down at the kitchen table, prayed for him, and gave him the gospel. It turned out that he had accepted Christ as a young boy but had drifted from God as an adult. Our conversation was the encouragement he needed as he started down a difficult road that would, unfortunately, include divorce. Later, he started attending our church and came back to the Lord.

Unlike Al, Stacey was very cold and hard-hearted. But I mustered my courage and called her on the phone. I said, "Stacey, I know what's happened with you and Al. I just want you to know that we're here for you. If there's anything we can do, just let us know." She thanked me and hung up.

Not long after that, we found out her two boys had chicken pox, and she couldn't stay home with them because she had to go to work. So I offered to watch them for her.

That first morning at her house, I went into her bathroom and found her toilet black with mold and crud. I went back home to find some cleanser and cleaned her toilet until it shone.

Somehow, I know my offer to help with her kids softened Stacey. And the fact that I cleaned the toilet seemed to impact her greatly. Our church was having a retreat soon where we planned to watch Focus on the Family films. I invited her and, lo and behold, she and her boys came with me. At that retreat, Stacey accepted Christ. We were overjoyed!

Through the years, Stacey has been up and down, in and out with God. But she has continued to pursue Him. She is now a delightful person with a wonderful personality. Stacey was the kind of person of whom my other neighbors would say, "Becky, why don't you just give up on her?" Well, what if I had? ■

Taking a Risk

Neighborhoods can include unsavory people and scary situations. Those high fences and closed doors don't always keep private the sounds of angry shouting or even physical abuse. It's also not uncommon today, regardless of the type of neighborhood, to have known or suspected drug dealers living close by.

Why would we as Christians want to get in the middle of all that? It would be much less complicated to just tend to our own families and protect ourselves from the world around us.

When you open your heart and home to your neighborhood, you'll encounter people in difficult, ugly, or even dangerous circumstances. Your home may become a magnet for people who are hurting. What could be more Christlike than that?

You read the first part of Michael Southern's story in chapter 3, from Norm's point of view (he's the fellow Norm met at OfficeMax). Many testimonies end at the point when the person prays to receive Christ. But as any Christian knows, the battle doesn't end there.

Now, read on as Michael shares his struggles and triumphs as a new Christian, following his decision to receive Christ that December morning in a Littleton restaurant. Keep in mind that this whole story occurred in upper-middle class, suburban Denver—a very typical, "safe" neighborhood.

Michael:

There was no question in my mind that something had changed that morning when I prayed with Norm. I felt as if I had been freed from all the stress and anger on my shoulders. I look back today and know it was my moment of salvation. But people don't just walk away cleanly from dealing drugs and running with the kinds of people I ran with. I still had a lot of baggage.

New Year's was coming, and I had friends who wanted to celebrate. I ended up going on a month-long partying binge—drugs, booze, you name it. All that time, Norm was trying to get in contact with me. I found out later that he cried in the middle of the night out of concern for me because he didn't know where I was.

Norm eventually came to my house one night and found me partying with friends. I was standing there drinking a beer and smoking a cigarette. I thought I knew what he would say: "Now that Christ is in your life, you don't need this stuff to give you pleasure and help you relax." I'd always thought Christians were "Don't drink, don't smoke, goody-two-shoes" people. That was what society had told me. But even though Norm didn't approve of my choices, he wasn't the least bit critical or judgmental. I relaxed and felt free to introduce him to my friends. Norm spent quite a bit of time talking to my friends that night and even led one of them in a prayer to accept Christ. After a while, he left, and I continued to party.

I had no doubt that my salvation experience was real. But the problems in my life pushed it into the background. In those next days and weeks, my friends and I continued to deal drugs from our house.

One day after coming home from work, I was going to the bathroom, and I heard a voice. I looked around and saw a gun in front of my head. It was a Drug Enforcement Administration (DEA) agent.

"Freeze," he said. "Finish what you're doing and meet me in the kitchen."

"Son," he said in the kitchen, "do you know what I could bust you for?"

"No," I said. "Drinking, maybe?"

"We've seen the drug activity that circulates in and out of this house," he told me. "All we need is a search warrant and we can come back."

I had thirty bags of marijuana in the freezer and a plastic bag of cocaine hidden in a flowerpot in my bedroom. I also had razors, scales, and other stuff. I was relieved; I could have been majorly busted that day. The agent left his card. He'd driven the point home.

I thought, *I've accepted Christ, but I don't know how to get out of this lifestyle. This Christianity stuff is great and all, but is it really going to change anything?*

Norm kept trying to contact me, but I'd canceled phone service for fear of the police and DEA. I was paranoid, looking over my shoulder, looking out the window when I got home. The cops came to my house searching for me a couple of times. They had arrest warrants on me for writing bad checks, aiding and abetting a felon, a DUI hit-and-run, and a bunch of other stuff. My friends told them they hadn't seen me.

I planned to leave Colorado in another week or two to take the heat off. In the meantime, my friends and I still partied. I went on a crystal-meth binge.

Finally, everything came to a head one Saturday night. We were going to kill someone—a kid who had double-crossed us in a drug deal. My friend set it all up. We were going to tie this kid to a chair, douse him with gasoline, and light him on fire. But we were so wasted on crystal meth and Southern Comfort that we fell asleep.

I awoke to three guys hitting me—the kid we were going to kill and two of his friends. They had broken into my house, looking to beat up my friend, and had found me first. My friend ran to get his gun and fired point-blank at one of the guys. The bullet grazed off his head and hit a wall.

They bolted, and we took off after them on foot. We hadn't gotten very far when the cops pulled up, recognized us, and told us to freeze. They handcuffed me facedown on the pavement in front of a gas station. I was so wasted I was almost in a blackout stage. Turns out I had a .34 blood-alcohol content. They had all these warrants on me, so I went to jail.

That's where Norm and I met up again. I called him Sunday morning from the Jefferson County Jail. I didn't have anybody else to call. I don't think my mom and dad could have handled it.

Norm visited me almost every day in jail. That's where I really learned how to pray—after I finally accepted the fact that I was behind bars. The only thing I had in there was the Word of God and prayer. Norm also gave me a booklet called *How to Experience God's Love and Forgiveness.*

I asked Norm to call my dad for me. Dad didn't know about any of this, and I was afraid of his anger. Norm went to see him, and they discovered they'd been classmates at Denver South High School thirty-four years earlier. They struck up a friendship and also came up with a plan to get me out of jail.

God blessed the whole situation. My lawyer, my dad, and Norm vouched for me in front of the judge, and Norm said he would personally take total responsibility for me. So I was released. And I was transformed. Norm took a picture of me smiling and pointing toward heaven in front of the jail. But there was still some work to be done in me. I had damaged myself, both physically and spiritually.

I was in Norm's care. I'd lost everything in my house, and the house itself was trashed. My so-called friends had gone on a binge and torn the place up. My parents had just separated, so I lived in their empty house for a short time. I got a job cutting grass at a golf course. And I was having bad nosebleeds and migraines, the lingering effects of drug use.

There I was, out from behind bars, cleaned up, Jesus in my heart. But I was still a mess. Accepting reality was worse than being on drugs. I continued to struggle within. When my parents' house sold, Norm and Becky invited me to move in with them. ■

Norm and Becky:

We had been thinking about this for a long time. We lived in an apartment when we met Michael. Eight months later, we bought a home. In the meantime, we met three of Michael's friends—a man and two young women—who were all brand-new Christians. To make a long story short, they all ended up living with us for the summer. This wasn't something that we impulsively decided. We had prayed about it and talked it through. When God moves like this, He gives a sense of boldness and peace. ■

Michael:

Even though I was living with Norm and Becky, I still had contact with some friends from my past. I'd party with them and get high maybe once every two weeks. I just didn't understand about getting that out of my life. Even the relatively small habits, such as smoking, were hard to change. Becky knew that. When she saw me one day in the yard smoking a cigarette, her disappointment and frustration about everything finally came out. She started to cry. Then she said, "Let's just sit down and pray about everything—drugs, cigarettes, drinking—and get all that stuff out of your life. You are a new creation in Christ." So we prayed, and I finally got serious about Christ.

Not long after that, Becky took me to a golf course to practice. She knew I loved golf, and she wanted to watch me play. I had played in high school and was a pretty good athlete. I was hitting golf balls on the driving range, and it started to rain. I hadn't swung a club in five years, but I was hitting them better than I ever had. I wondered, *God, what are You doing in my life?* Becky sat there in the rain, watching me for hours.

Finally, she went up to the restaurant, where she bumped into some people she knew from Colorado Christian University in Denver. They were preparing for a ninety-one-hole golf fund-raiser in two days. Becky saw the golf coach, Brian Fort, and asked, "What would it take for an individual to get on your golf team? I know this really neat guy you've got to meet."

When I finished hitting and went up to the restaurant to find Becky, she introduced me to Coach Fort. He asked what my handicap was, and I said, "Well, I haven't played in five years." Then he wanted to know about my grades and said I'd need to show him ACT or SAT scores. "But before you do any of that," he said, "if you can raise five hundred dollars, you can play in the golf tournament Friday."

Where was I going to get five hundred dollars? Norm and Becky said, "C'mon. Trust God. It will work out." They started calling some friends in their church and Bible studies, and they raised the money in two days.

I still hadn't played a round in five years. But that day, I played ninety-one holes, hit great shots, and finished ten under par. The coach said, "Anytime you want to play on the golf team, just let me know. Take that ACT and get going."

I spent that whole summer interviewing and taking tests. People laughed at me and said I'd never make it. But Norm and Becky kept telling me, "We'll prove them wrong."

After what seemed like an endless run of studying and tests, I got accepted to CCU. I was overjoyed and also scared. I couldn't believe I was really in college. On top of that, I was awarded a golf scholarship. The school had been looking for an opportunity to give a chance to disadvantaged students who showed heart. (In fact, today at CCU they call those students "Mike Southerns.")

My coach and my professors were great. They built me up day after day. I was growing in the Lord and feeling great about college. But as I got into the semester, I also began hearing about keg parties—not on campus, but in apartments close to campus. I met people who were great Christian guys, but you could tell they partied and were wild. God blessed me, though. He really kept me away from that crowd and gave me godly friendships, especially on the golf team and with Coach Fort.

In the fall of my junior year, I had a setback. I was living with Norm and Becky again for a semester. Some Christian friends and I went out after work. Then we went back to one guy's place, where he had a bong and some marijuana. And it just caught me. I got very high and drank a lot of wine. When I got home at about 1:00 A.M., I confessed to Norm and Becky: "I've been partying tonight. I've done wrong, and I need your forgiveness." ■

Norm and Becky:

We forgave Michael, and many tears were shed. We prayed with him and sent him out the next day to make things right at school. ■

Michael:

CCU and the golf team had rules. One was, *no drugs.* I didn't feel good about breaking the rules, and I knew I needed to turn myself in. I talked to the coach and to the dean of students and told them I was all right with whatever they did. They didn't kick me out, although Coach did suspend me for a couple of meets. Instead, they forgave me and gave me a break.

Five years after that "chance" encounter at the golf course in May 2001, I graduated with a degree in communications. I became the first person in my immediate family to graduate from college.

Today, I work at Home Depot in Littleton and teach Sunday school and usher at church. Who'd have ever thought that I'd be a teacher? I've been able to share my testimony with kids many times and talk about the lessons I've learned. I can give insight and wisdom to them. I'm trying to leave a legacy like the Wretlinds have.

Norm and Becky helped me turn my life around—just as they have for many others—but they've seen their share of disappointments, too. They have been let down by people who accepted Christ and then went in the wrong direction, including two of my friends who lived with us that first summer. But wherever they are today, they know that Norm and Becky love them, and so does God. Scripture is simple—"[God] will never leave you nor forsake you" (Deuteronomy 31:6,8; Joshua 1:5). Maybe He just hasn't written their success stories yet.

I had two choices the day I first met Norm at OfficeMax: respond to his kindness or reject him. Where would I be today if Norm had just gone to church that following Sunday morning, December 17, 1995, instead of meeting me for breakfast? I'd be a twenty-eight-year-old guy strung out on drugs, very desperate, very sad, and maybe even imprisoned or dead. ■

OPENING YOUR HOME

Michael's gradual transformation taught us another thing about the way God works in our neighbors: He doesn't give up on them, even when they appear hopeless.

We think of Michael as our real-life parable of the Good Samaritan. We met him along the path, half dead. We took him in, nursed his wounds, and in essence adopted him as our son. Loving neighbors means not only giving them the gospel, but giving your own life as well. That has an impact beyond what a Bible study can do.

Often when Christians encounter hurting people, we think only about referring them to a professional counselor, a pregnancy center, or a shelter. But why not also invite them into your Christian family setting and show them "God with skin on"? Millions of sincere, mature Christians have rooms in their homes that they don't use. Their homes are stable. Their lives are stable. Their needs are met. Especially to those couples whose nests are empty, or partially empty, we say: Be open to using your home to minister to others.

There's a certain amount of natural fear in opening our homes to this. Something bad could happen. We've had things stolen, things broken, people stumbling home drunk or high. Yes, precautions must be taken, boundaries held firmly, and accountability established. But we shouldn't let fear keep us from getting close to "scary" neighbors.

We must see the bigger picture. Remember what 1 John 4:18 tells us: "There is no fear in love. But perfect love drives out fear." We have the God of the universe to protect us. Safety is not about building ourselves a fort and protecting our families and our possessions. Safety is being at the center of God's will.

We are often reminded, too, that not every person we help will end up like Michael Southern. In the Parable of the Sower, Jesus' story gives us several snapshots of people met along life's path (see Matthew 13:1-23). In our neighborhoods, the people we meet will respond differently to Christian love and hospitality, depending on the state of their "soil."

Over the years, we have sown much seed into many different types of soil. We have rejoiced over seeing a few seeds take root and grow and even reproduce. We have also borne the pain of being rejected by some people, being taken advantage of by others, and having our hearts broken by those who returned to their old bondage. That pain is intense for us because we have invested so much love and hope in these people. But we also are encouraged by the realization that the soil of people's lives can change. Our job is to sow the seed everywhere we can cultivate the soil and leave the results to God.

This kind of lifestyle, of course, will change the dynamic of your home, your marriage, and your family. In the next chapter, we'll look at the powerful impact that is created when a Christian family focuses on their neighborhood.

CHAPTER TEN

A Family Affair: Leaving a Legacy

"All the families of the earth will be blessed through you."

Genesis 12:3, nlt

Almost everything we have discussed about neighborhood outreach up to this point could apply to any believer, regardless of status: single, married, kids, no kids, living in an apartment, or living in single-family housing. Loving Christians can always leave a legacy of changed lives.

Now we would like to focus on the unique opportunities that Christian families have. God not only places parents in the neighborhood, but He also places the entire family there. That includes kids, dogs, cats, and maybe even a gerbil or two. As parents reach out to care for their neighbors, children usually develop a heart for the lost as well. They in turn will continue to pass this passion on to their future families. That's how it works.

Do you and your spouse have goals for your marriage and family? Typically, for Christians those goals include a happy, loving marriage; raising children who love God; creating a warm, safe, comfortable home; being fulfilled in careers; and attaining financial stability. Obviously, there's nothing wrong with any of those. The list strikes us as incomplete, though. Families could strive for so much more.

God brought you together as husband and wife to create a picture of Christ's love for the church (see Ephesians 5:22-33) and perhaps to create a family with children. He also brought you together because of the way your spiritual gifts can be used in combination to serve and honor Him.

The two of us are definitely opposites in many areas. Norm has the gift of evangelism and Becky the gifts of hospitality and mercy. As we have learned to walk in step with the Holy Spirit, we have discovered a dynamic synergy that enables both of us to impact others for Christ far beyond what we could do alone. We've learned that we can accomplish more when we combine our gifts. A friend of ours once quipped, "Norm catches the fish and Becky cleans them."

God wants your whole family to pursue a common goal that's bigger than your individual goals. Sure, you want a happy family, but what is the *purpose* of that happy family? Ask yourselves: What would happen if we as a family loved our neighbors together? If we let the neighbors see and experience how we live as a Christian family? Would it give our marriage a greater spiritual focus? Would we take personal holiness more seriously? Would our family devotional and prayer times take on more meaning? Would our children—especially if they're teenagers—see a higher purpose for their lives than everything being "me-centered"?

While our daughters, Mindi and Miriam, were growing up in our Texas neighborhood, they played a big role in what God did there. In a neighborhood full of young families, children gave the adults points of connection via school, sports, clubs, or simply playing together in back-yards. Often, their friendships would trigger a chain of events that resulted in a parent or a whole family coming to Christ—sometimes quickly, sometimes not until years later.

Mindi, for example, led her friend Karoline to Christ on the school playground when they were both five years old. Mindi couldn't wait to tell us, and we all rejoiced together. The two girls remained friends through much of their childhood. Karoline came from a dysfunctional home dominated by alcoholism, so she spent a lot of time in our home as she grew up. We prayed together often for her family. About five years ago during a visit to Texas, we saw Karoline and her mother, Alyce.

"I know the Lord now because of all your prayers," Alyce told us with tears in her eyes. "I used to be so upset with you because I knew you were praying for me. Now, I can't tell you enough what it means to me that you were living there in the neighborhood, loving my daughter. I was an alco-holic at the time, and I didn't want you praying for me. I was too proud. But I've really been humbled. And now I'm walking with God."

Mindi:

We always had the attitude that we were ministering to other people. Our house was always open; people felt welcome anytime. Our friends were always made to feel like adopted children in the home. Growing up around that, with my parents always reaching out to people, I developed that same attitude. I can remember many times when my parents talked with the neighbors out in the yard or when people came by the house and Mom and Dad talked with them. My sister and I knew they were talking to them about the Lord. As we got older, we'd pray for the people during those conversations. ■

Becky:

Family Bible reading and prayer were foundational to what happened in Richardson. On many evenings right after dinner, our family would pray for our neighbors and the girls' schoolmates—some for specific needs, others more generally, but all for salvation. Those prayer times together made us sensitive to how God was involving us in work He had already begun. ■

Miriam:

We would all kneel in a line along the front of the couch. I loved that. That's how I learned to pray and how I caught Mom and Dad's heart for people. When we prayed together as a family, God brought opportunities or opened our eyes to something He was doing so that we could be involved and be used.

When I was twelve and my sister was ten, we were both baptized. Two neighborhood sisters, friends of ours through school, were exactly our ages. Their family didn't go to church. We were at their house one day, and they started asking us what it means to be baptized. I went out in the kitchen for something, and when I came back, they were all kneeling down. I was talking as I walked in, and Mindi said, "Shhh! We're praying." She was leading them both in a prayer for salvation. ■

Becky:

The mother of those two girls had attended some of the neighborhood parties, and I had played tennis with her. She was eager for our daughters to be friends. She had accepted Christ as a child but had ended up in an abusive and spiritually broken marriage. She had begun to reach out to me for counsel and comfort; that's why our girls were at her house that day. After her girls accepted Christ, she ended up recommitting her life, as well.

Those kinds of interactions sometimes raise questions about what's appropriate and respectful to neighborhood families of other faiths. What if, for instance, your children are talking about Christ with a Jewish or Muslim child? Should you encourage your kids to lead their friend in a prayer for salvation without the parents knowing about it? Should *adults* witness to neighborhood kids without their parents knowing about it? Generally, we have taken the approach that kids minister to kids, adults to adults.

Starting in about second grade, Mindi had a friend who was Jewish. The two girls walked to school together. During the course of their daily conversations, they talked about Jewish traditions, such as Hanukkah, and also about what Mindi believed. One day Mindi told her that if she didn't accept Jesus, she wouldn't go to heaven.

That comment got back to another Jewish mother in our neighborhood, a friend of the little girl's mother. She called me and bawled me out, saying I should tell Mindi she shouldn't be talking to her friend's daughter about religion. I replied, "I would never want to offend your friend and her daughter, so I hope you won't take it that way. I didn't tell Mindi to talk to her, and I didn't tell her not to talk to her. That's just children talking. I don't think there's much harm done."

After all, the little girl told Mindi about her traditions, also. And as it turned out, there was no long-term tension over the matter. The girl's mother never said anything about it to me. And the woman who called to complain later wanted to be friends. ■

A LOVING FAMILY

As our daughters grew up, it meant a lot to them that we loved and cared for their friends who were having problems. And oh, were there problems! For every family who came to Christ in that neighborhood, at least one other family was an absolute mess: marriages on the rocks, alcoholic parents, adultery, kids on drugs, homosexuality, even satanism. Our girls felt as though they could invite anyone over and he or she would feel welcome in our house. A lot of their friends called us Mom and Dad. Their homes lacked loving nurture and God's presence.

Miriam:

In high school, I was a drum major. One of the girls in our band was killed in a car accident involving another band member who was driving drunk. It happened two blocks from our house. The whole band was in shock. They looked to my family for help because they knew my dad was a religious "pastor man." We shared the gospel openly with those high school kids who were so brokenhearted. It wasn't a forced, uncomfortable thing at all. My friends invited our family into this situation. They needed to feel God's love.

After that, we started a band Bible study at our house. Through that, at least three girls came to Christ. It was great to be able to offer hope so naturally.

Over the years, a lot of kids wanted to be at my house and near my parents. My mom would always serve them food, for one thing, but she and

Dad were excellent listeners, too. These kids knew my parents were interested in their lives. That was our identity as a family together. ■

WE HAVE WHAT THEY NEED

Crisis situations present opportunities to help neighbors find God. In fact, we pray regularly that God will make us aware of our neighbors' crises and spiritual needs. That doesn't make us spiritual ambulance chasers; we simply love our neighbors and reach out to those who need healing, just as Jesus did. We have what they need.

During our girls' teen years, we consciously decided to drop some of our activities. Norm changed to a job that didn't require so many hours and so much travel. This was just too important a time in the life of our family. We needed to walk alongside our girls. Norm and the girls had alternating father-daughter "dates" once every two weeks. Once a week, we'd have a family night where we'd talk about what was going on in each other's lives, do fun activities or crafts, and pray together. That helped us stay connected no matter how busy we were keeping up with our everyday schedules.

Parents of teenagers tend to say, "I'm going to dread these years." But they can really enjoy them. We were involved in all of the girls' school and church functions, and we always encouraged them to invite their friends over. When they came over, we paid attention to them and got to know them because we realized not all of them were getting attention at home. We also got to know the guys our daughters liked and hung around with. That was a protection for the girls and a way to share Christ with the nonChristian boys.

IT TAKES COMMITMENT

The neighbor child who was part of our family over the longest period of time was a girl we'll call Tammy. She was at our house often, especially during her elementary-school years. She accepted Christ at our church. Her mother had become a Christian as a child, but at the time we were helping nurture Tammy, the family was extremely dysfunctional, with a lot of angry outbursts. Tammy found security in our home.

We tried to help Tammy as she progressed through high school and later as she got involved with drinking and affairs, following the example her mom had set after divorcing her abusive dad. One Christmas, Tammy and her mom had no place to go, so they lived with us through the holidays. Their lifestyle was wild, but we decided not to be judgmental. Instead, we showed unconditional love and let them be themselves. Many times, they both were in tears over feeling loved and not condemned.

We kept in touch with Tammy over the years, and she and her mom both ended up coming back to the Lord. We as a family even informally "adopted" Tammy as our third daughter. She came to us for guidance and counsel when she was dating and later engaged to be married. In fact, Norm performed the wedding—some fifteen years after we first met her. Through a very personal, long-term, nurturing relationship, two lives were transformed.

Truly loving your neighbors takes time, energy, and an intense spiritual commitment. As Christians, we are engaged in a spiritual battle. It can't help but affect you, your marriage, and your kids. It will change the dynamics of your home for God's glory.

On Christmas morning in 1976, we got an emergency call from the mother of one of Mindi's friends. The father, who was dying of cancer, had just been rushed to the hospital. Could Norm come to see him? Sure, it disrupted our family's Christmas morning a little. But Mindi loved this friend so much, and she was excited for her dad to go. We all were. Norm had the privilege of leading this man to the Lord. The man died just a few weeks later.

This was, and is, our life as a family. It's not just an added-on thing. We experienced sorrow and frustration when people we cared deeply about went through difficult times or turned away from God. That was overshadowed, though, when another neighbor began a personal relationship with Christ.

It's not that we never had tension. We went through some of the worst tension in our marriage during those years in Richardson as we learned how to blend our spiritual gifts and our home and work responsibilities. We were struggling, also, with personal and emotional problems from our past. God was working on our spiritual maturity at the same time He was using us to bring neighbors to Christ.

Becky:

When Mindi was a teenager, she once brought home a girl named Marcy. The two of them worked together at a Mexican restaurant, but Marcy was also a prostitute. The three of us sat around our kitchen table, and Mindi and I led her to Christ. She was a handful—very needy and unstable. She clung to our family and called us all the time. We loved her and tried our best to help her, but it was emotionally draining. I wasn't ready to have someone else living in my house at that point. It wouldn't have been the best situation for our family. As Marcy began to go to church with us, she began to meet other Christian friends. And I felt the freedom to ask those friends to reach out to her, also. Someone else in our church family helped her find a place to live. ■

KNOW YOUR LIMITS

The Holy Spirit, who places needy neighbors in your path and moves in your heart to minister to them, will also help you establish boundaries. It would have been wrong for us to forsake our marriage and family responsibilities in order to maximize the help we could give someone else. Hurting people need to see in us a balanced marriage and family, too. Their crisis should not create a crisis in our home. They also need to see that we are real people who have hurts, failures, and disappointments, just as they do. The difference they'll see is that we take those problems to the Lord in prayer.

One of the most difficult things about ministering to hurting people is realizing we will not be able to meet all of their needs. God places us in a position to do what we can, when we can. Jesus illustrated this in His parable of the Good Samaritan (see Luke 10:25-37). When the Samaritan encountered the hurting man in his path, he bandaged the man's wounds and took care of him. The next day, he took the man to an inn, gave the innkeeper money for the man's care, and then left. Jesus doesn't tell us if the Samaritan ever saw the wounded man again.

Scripture gives us guidelines for what we are responsible to do. As 1 John 3:17 says, "If anyone has material possessions and sees his brother in need but has no pity on him, how can the love of God be in him?" If we don't learn how to apply these guidelines, we can be out of balance. We must continually seek to have the mind of Christ, who said, "I tell you the truth, the Son can do nothing by himself; he can do only what he sees his Father doing, because whatever the Father does the Son also does" (John 5:19). In other words, as we draw close to God, He will guide us toward the work He wants us to do. He understands that we cannot help every needy, hurting person. He did not even ask that of Jesus.

Over the years, we have found that God doesn't place us in a position to minister to someone without giving us the time, energy, and resources to do so. But we have to stay focused on Him. The two of us, by nature, are all-or-nothing people. We give our all and then have nothing left for a while. We have gone beyond wise boundaries at times and have become exhausted. When we simply do what comes naturally—rescuing people—without consulting the Lord at every step, we can go beyond what is healthy for our physical bodies, our marriage, and our family.

Becky:

When Michael Southern was living with us, I often would help him with his college assignments. I would sometimes get so wrapped up in helping him at every step that I would exhaust myself. I would be useless for days as I recuperated—all because I had invested more time and energy than was really wise to give. ■

Miriam:

While I was growing up, the phone rang constantly, and there were always people at our house. I liked it. It was really exciting, and I didn't know anything different. But now that I've been married fifteen years and have been away from that, I can honestly say that it would be too much for me now. I probably would get really stressed out. Right now, especially with young children in our home, I'm trying to learn the balance of having a lifestyle of reaching out, while at the same time having boundaries. ■

LEAVING A LEGACY

We've seen how a loving Christian family can transform a neighborhood and future generations. Many of the children from our Texas neighborhood grew up learning the importance of reaching out to hurting people and telling them about Christ. Today, as parents themselves, they have transplanted that mindset to many other neighborhoods.

In our daughters' cases, those ministries bear some resemblance to what they grew up experiencing, but there are differences, too.

Miriam:

Before my husband and I had children, I felt a strong calling for mission work. We were overseas for a little while. And then when my husband was in medical school, we had an evangelistic Christmas party with some of his classmates. Since then, because of his career, our ministry has been very different from the one I grew up around. We've been in North Carolina for two years now, and it's really the first time in fifteen years of marriage that we've settled down. I'm relearning how to interact and be natural with our neighbors. ■

Mindi:

When my husband and I were first married, I had a strong desire to have the kind of neighborly ministry I grew up with. We haven't had the great success my parents have, but through the two neighborhood parties we've hosted, one neighbor from each has come to the Lord. Overall, there's a ministry mindset in our family—that God loves the lost and wants us to love them, befriend them, and reach out to them. I don't think I would have that attitude if I hadn't grown up in the home I did. ■

Norm and Becky:

We believe that our family's history is really *"His* story." In our living room today, you'll find a basket filled with stones—memory stones. We got the idea from Joshua 4. God commanded the Israelites to pile up stones at the spot where He parted the Jordan river and allowed them to cross. The stones would serve as a memorial for what God had done there, bringing His people into the Promised Land.

Over the years, when a significant event would happen in our family, we would find a smooth stone and record the event with a permanent marker. Some of the stones in our basket read:

- Valentine's coffee, Stacey Court (our street in Richardson): Mary Pat accepted Christ, 1974.
- Karoline, Oct. 2, 1974: accepted Christ with Mindi in Dartmouth School yard.
- Michael Southern—met at OfficeMax, Dec. 14, 1995. Accepted Christ at Village Inn restaurant Dec. 17, 1995.

- Miriam rolled off a mountainside in her car in a blizzard. God stopped the car on its side with a little pine tree. October 1984.

There are many others. The great thing is that we can pick up those stones at any time and recall the spiritual history of our family.

Many Christian families become ineffective at reaching neighbors for the reasons that Jesus talked about in Mark 4:19: "The worries of this life, the deceitfulness of wealth and the desires for other things come in and choke the word, making it unfruitful." The joyous Christian family is the one who sees itself as a lighthouse for its neighborhood. The children learn to focus not just on themselves and what they may succeed at some-day, but on the fact that God, right now, has given them the privilege of being lights in this dark world. That is success in God's eyes. It brings a sense of unity to a family, and it helps children see the bigger picture—knowing the *real* purpose of marriage and family life. What higher purpose could there be than helping people experience the love of God?

CHAPTER ELEVEN

PUTTING IT ALL TOGETHER

*The entire law is summed up in a single command: "Love your neigh-
bor as yourself."*   GALATIANS 5:14

All of the stories you've read in this book can be traced to the two major
points we mentioned early on. The first principle is that the Great
Commission is fulfilled when Christians live out the Great Commandment:
Love your neighbor as yourself.

It's all about living Christ in full view of your neighborhood, making
your neighbors a priority, and intentionally establishing friendships, even
if it costs you time and energy. When you show warm, Christian love to
neighbors, you will impact them in ways that might not be apparent until
much later. Jerry Ryan's statement from chapter 8 could be echoed by
many, many people who came to faith because of a neighbor's witness: "I
felt the warmth before I saw the light."

We hope and pray that this book has inspired you to connect with
your neighbors. You may already be planning a neighborhood get-
together, be it a summer barbecue, a Christmas party, or for some other
occasion. God may be telling you to establish stronger relationships with

individual neighbors, too. You might decide to follow some of our practical steps for breaking the ice. Or maybe you'll come up with creative ideas of your own. You will be most effective ministering to people in ways that are uniquely yours.

Before you do any of that, though, ask yourself: *Is this desire in my head or in my heart? Do I want to reach my neighbors because it's what I should do or because that is who I am in Christ?* It's the difference between obeying Christ out of obligation and serving Him wholeheartedly because that is your spiritual identity. As Paul wrote in Galatians 2:20, "I have been crucified with Christ and I no longer live, but Christ lives in me."

For those who are motivated to love their neighbors because that is their identity in Christ, there's a huge payoff: joy! It may be as simple as the smile you receive from a neighbor after you've stopped and said hello in the front yard. Or it may be the unspeakable joy you feel from leading someone to Christ.

For us, it's been the joy of Mary Pat Parma, who knocked on our front door to tell Becky she had just prayed to accept Jesus . . . the joy of Jeanne Ryan calling to tell us she had prayed and knew for sure she was going to heaven . . . the joy of watching God transform Michael Southern from a hopeless druggie into a radiant young man who loves Jesus with all his heart. And it's been the joy of having some of our neighbors walk to church with us and seeing them cry during the service because they are so overcome by the love of God.

Joy like that makes every heartache and every potential rejection worth the risk. As the apostle Paul wrote, "I consider that our present sufferings are not worth comparing with the glory that will be revealed in us" (Romans 8:18). When neighbors respond to us, it is like a glimpse of heaven. Our lives have value because we give them to others.

Do you truly love your neighbors as you love yourself? Have you taken time to prayerfully consider what that means? Have you thought about the fact that both Jesus and Paul considered this command central to the Christian life? We can say with absolute confidence that God's primary will for you as a believer is to love your neighbors. Remember that the motivation for all of this is God's unconditional love for *us*.

Above all, commit to praying for your neighborhood. Prayer is the catalyst for everything else that will happen. It keeps you spiritually alert and helps you see your neighbors from God's point of view. Do you want passion for reaching them? Ask God to give you a burden for those He is drawing to Himself. Then befriend them and watch in amazement at what happens.

USING WHAT GOD GAVE YOU

Our second undergirding principle is this: Successful witnessing happens when Christians take the initiative to befriend nonChristians, share their experiences of Christ with them, depend on the power of the Holy Spirit, and leave the results to God. You say you don't have the gift of evangelism? Most Christians don't. So identify and use your own particular gifts to love your neighbors. God uses all believers and all spiritual gifts—teaching, mercy, hospitality, helps, and so on—to save the lost. Your ability to strike up conversations and host parties isn't the issue. The heart of evangelism is not the verbal message but rather the love and kindness you show to others. You may never give your testimony at a party, but you can certainly love your neighbors.

Now, that said, don't sell yourself short, either. Regardless of your gifts and your personality, fully expect and anticipate that you can help someone accept Christ. Our prayer through the years has been, "We want to lead someone to you, Lord. Please give us the opportunities and the courage to do so." And He has. If you resign yourself to never having that opportunity, you will miss out on the most joyful experience you could ever have.

WINNING THE RIGHT TO BE HEARD

As we bring this book to a close, let us introduce you to one more person: Dr. Bill Brewer, our dear friend and pastor of Richland Bible Fellowship Church. Bill has been our personal mentor and a great encourager over the years. His faithful shepherding of those original neighbors in Richardson caused the impact of that movement to grow and expand in ways we'll never know here on earth.

Bill:

People in our church have said, "I don't have the gift of evangelism like Norm and Becky. They walk up to somebody in a store, they share Christ, the people trust Christ, and then they disciple them for six months or the people move in with them. I could never do that!"

What we tell them is that God didn't make them Norm and Becky Wretlind. Every person's style will differ, based on the way God wired that individual. We all have the responsibility to learn the gospel, flesh it out in our lives, and then share it. We all need to be capable of sharing the words of the gospel. But we need to do it within the context of our own personal styles and gifts. Some people, for example, may have the gift of hospitality or "helps." They can be involved in the process of evangelism by hosting a party. They don't have to be the person who stands up and actually explains the message.

Evangelism has been defined as helping and encouraging people to move one step closer to faith in Christ. That's a process. We tend to think of evangelism only in terms of the result. Jesus said some will plant, some will water, and some will reap the harvest, but all will rejoice together because they were all a part of that process (see John 4).

Neighborly evangelism is not knocking on doors and trying to push the Bible down people's throats. It's being a neighbor first and loving people into the kingdom. It's being with them in their pain and suffering and hardships, and not closing our doors to them. It's modeling the love of Christ and winning the right to be heard. And then, when the time is right, when the soil of their hearts is receptive, the seed can be planted.

A friend of mine from church, Jeff Branch, decided he was going to invite his neighbor, Gary, to hear Billy Graham. Jeff was outside working on his truck, and Gary came over to chat. In the course of their conversation, out of the blue, Jeff said, "Hey, have you ever heard of Billy Graham?"

"Yeah, I've heard of him," Gary replied. "He's an evangelist, right?"

"That's right," Jeff said. "He's going to be at Texas Stadium next week. I'm going to go on Thursday night. Would you like to go with me?"

Gary nodded and said, "Yeah. I think I would."

Jeff was shocked. He hadn't expected him to say yes.

While Jeff was celebrating the fact that Gary had agreed to go, another neighbor from across the street came over. Jeff thought, *Hey, it worked once, maybe it'll work again.* So he went through the same conversation.

The guy said, "Why in the hell would I want to go hear Billy Graham?"

They talked about other things for a few minutes, and the guy left. Jeff thought, *Oh well, one out of two isn't bad.*

On Thursday night, Jeff and Gary went to the crusade, and when Billy

Graham gave the invitation, Gary walked down to the floor and prayed to receive Christ. He came to church the next Sunday and has been in church every Sunday since. His faith is growing by leaps and bounds.

Jeff *lived* the gospel message in front of his neighbor for years, and he won the right to be heard. Then he simply invited Gary to go to an event. It could have been a Christmas party, a Billy Graham crusade, a concert, or whatever. Gary trusted Christ at that moment in time because God had prepared his heart. ■

A LEGACY OF FAITH

That's the story, and it goes on and on. When people come to Christ, it's almost always because of the influence of a friend or a relative—a person who loved them, pursued them, and enabled them to hear the gospel.

When we go back and tell those stories, the legacy of faith continues. In Richardson, some of those original couples' kids are now in leadership positions in the same church. It's exciting to see the generational impact of someone sharing Christ with his or her neighbor, seeing that neighbor come to faith, and then seeing the neighbor's family come to faith. That amazing multiplication process has continued for almost thirty years in that neighborhood.

God has a story in mind for your neighborhood, too. Our deepest longing is that all of our brothers and sisters in Christ will take part in creating these joyful stories, with this as our common thread: We loved our neighbors as ourselves.

CHRISTMAS PARTY ICEBREAKER GAMES

WHO OR WHAT AM I?

You can play this as your party guests begin to arrive. As each guest signs the guest book, place a sticker on his or her back. Each sticker will contain a word or phrase associated with your party's theme or holiday event. For instance, for a Fourth of July party, stickers might say "Thomas Jefferson," "1776," "fireworks," and so on; for a Christmas party: "Scrooge," "Santa Claus," or "eggnog."

Your guests may ask each person only three questions as they try to figure out what their stickers say. They can ask only questions that have "yes" or "no" answers (such as, "Am I a person?" or "Am I a food item?"). When they guess who or what they are, they move the label to their front. Encourage everyone to complete the game before moving on to the next event.

CHRISTMAS CAROL QUIZ

Divide your guests into groups of four or five people. Ask guests to "count off" to form their groups (this ensures they won't simply congregate with people they already know). Give a copy of the Christmas carol clues and a pen to each group and call, "Start." The first group to correctly guess all of the titles or phrases wins.

Clues

1. White metallic bellows
2. A quiet evening
3. Happiness on earth
4. A fat man in a red suit coming from the North Pole
5. Cards the corridors with branches of berries
6. One letter missing from the alphabet
7. A running event through thick, white stuff
8. Small city in Israel
9. The two of us, plus one male crowned ruler
10. It arrived at 12 A.M., uncluttered
11. Listen, the ushered nondevils are musically speaking
12. I must see my dentist before December 25
13. Far off in a barn
14. Ice cold, the white flakes male
15. Hallowed evening
16. I peeked at Mom smooching with a fat man in a red suit
17. Gather everyone, see Yellowstone Park
18. A certain bird in a tree

Answers

1. Silver Bells 2. Silent Night 3. Joy to the World 4. Santa Claus Is Coming to Town 5. Deck the halls with boughs of holly 6. Noel 7. Dashing through the snow 8. O Little Town of Bethlehem 9. We Three Kings 10. It Came upon the Midnight Clear 11. Hark! The Herald Angels Sing 12. All I Want for Christmas Is My Two Front Teeth 13. Away in a Manger 14. Frosty the Snowman 15. O Holy Night 16. I Saw Mommy Kissing Santa Claus 17. O Come, All Ye Faithful 18. A partridge in a pear tree

Variation: Have guests take a holiday trivia quiz. Quizzes for any season or holiday can be found easily on the Internet. Use a search engine like google.com, and type in the kind of quiz you're looking for. Example: "Valentine's Day trivia quiz."

GETTING-TO-KNOW-YOU BINGO

Prepare in advance one bingo sheet for each guest. Provide pencils. Guests ask one another questions from the bingo sheet. They may ask only three questions of each person before going on to another guest. If the question is true of the person, he or she signs the appropriate box. The winner is the first person to get five names in a row or diagonally. Use the following example to create your own bingo sheet customized for your group.

Who has lived in a foreign country?	Who is/was a teacher?	Who has played an instrument in band?	Who is a handyman?	Who has grandchildren?
Who is an engineer?	Who travels often in his/her occupation?	Who is attending college now?	Who has a nickname?	Who knows how to fix computers?
Who has kids under age four?	Who has moved in the past year?	Who received an e-mail in the past two days?	Who loves country music?	Who likes to work on cars?
Who has remodeled recently?	Who enjoys hiking?	Who is active in church?	Who had a garage sale last summer?	Who has a clean garage?
Who has put in a new lawn?	Who is/was a professional salesperson?	Who has lived on the East Coast?	Who enjoys biking?	Who earned a letter in high school sports?

TIPS FOR WRITING A TESTIMONY

Your personal testimony is a natural introduction to sharing the gospel. Use these guidelines to tell about what God has done in your life.

1. Let God be original in you. You have your own story to tell, and in the telling, Jesus Christ can be lifted up and glorified. Ask God to give you insight into how He has worked in your life.

2. Approach this as if you were chatting with an individual one-on-one rather than addressing a group. That will make your testimony more personal and natural. You don't need to be a polished speaker—just one who has been blessed by Christ and wants to share those blessings with another person.

3. As you write your story, avoid Christian terminology and jargon. A nonChristian may be perplexed by words such as *redeemed, sanctified, filled with the Spirit,* and so on. If you do use Christian terms, be sure to explain what they mean. Also, avoid using denominational names (Baptist, Presbyterian, and so on) because feelings about a particular church or denomination can sidetrack people from your point.

Before you begin writing, first read how the apostle Paul shared his story in Acts 22, 23, and 26. Note Paul's "before," "how," and "after." Organize your testimony accordingly.

Before I Trusted in Christ As My Savior

Spend a brief time on "before." This is not a biography from childhood. It's best to start at a time in your life that relates to your experience with Christ. If you became a Christian as a child, share some of your background that nonChristians can relate to, and then share a significant experience that shows how your life was before you truly acknowledged Christ as Lord of your life.

How I Came to Trust in Christ

Be specific. Use "who, what, when, where, and why" questions. The Holy Spirit often convinces people they should trust in Christ while others are talking about the process they went through. If the exact circumstances are unclear, simply share how you came to have assurance that Christ is in your life and heaven is your future home.

After I Began to Trust Christ for His Forgiveness and a New Beginning

Mention some ways you have experienced Christ working in your life. Be practical, realistic, and positive. Share specific changes He has brought about in your relationships with your spouse, children, and friends. Tell about specific victories over bad habits or bad attitudes. Discuss the impact on your life of obeying Scripture as your authority and trusting in Jesus Christ, who is alive today.

YOUR AFTER-PARTY QUESTIONNAIRE

Your experience in reaching out to your neighbors will inspire others to do the same. Therefore, please provide the information requested in this appendix and do the following:

1. Give this information to your church evangelism coordinator or your pastor. He or she will encourage others to host a party.

2. Mail a copy to NeighborHope Ministries, 11455 West Belleview Avenue, Littleton, CO 80127 or fill out the questionnaire on our website, at www.neighborhope.com. We'll use your information in our ongoing evangelistic research and literature.

Facts

Names of hosts:

Names of cohosts:

Day, date, and time of your party:

Focus of party (adults or children?):

Purpose of party (pre-evangelistic or evangelistic?):

Number of personally invited guests:

Number of guests who attended:

Feelings

Did you follow our "script" from this book, or did you use your own approach? What new ideas could you share?

Give a few highlights from your party.

How were the games and singing received?

What were the highlights of the sharing time?

What did you learn from the comment cards (if you used them)?

What changes would you make for future parties?

How did God work in you through this experience?

What do you sense God might be doing in the lives of your neighbors?

What ideas do you have that you might pursue next in your neighborhood?

What would help you be more effective in reaching your neighbors for Christ?

Thank you so much for your love and obedience to Christ. Your active love for your neighbors is helping to bring about the fulfillment of the Great Commission!

PLANNING SUGGESTIONS FOR

FUTURE MINISTRY TO NEIGHBORS

- Use a twelve-month planning calendar.
- If you hosted a Christmas party, write in any follow-up ideas you have for the next three months. Will you try to start a Bible study? Will you seek to befriend particular families on your block? Put their names in various months with an idea of what you might do together. Refer back to the list of ideas in chapter 2.
- Write in quality Christian events that might appeal to your neighbors (concerts, drama productions, and so on).
- Choose the month when you plan to have your next neighborhood party. That event will build on the current momentum. It is usually best to host gatherings in the summer and in December.

Resources

NeighborHope Ministries

NeighborHope Ministries was cofounded by Norm and Becky Wretlind. The organization's mission is to help equip all believers to fulfill their original calling: Love your neighbor as yourself. In doing so, Christians help fulfill the Great Commission right where they live. NeighborHope provides self-training tools for neighborhood evangelism and training seminars for churches across the United States. It is an active member of the Mission America Coalition. Further information is available on their website, at www.neighborhope.com.

Kingdom Building Ministries

Norm and Becky Wretlind do evangelism training and speaking around the nation through their partnership with Kingdom Building Ministries, an organization devoted to challenging, equipping, and mobilizing Christians to become active kingdom laborers.

> To receive more information about how you can schedule the Wretlinds to lead an evangelism-training workshop in your area or speak at your ministry event, visit Kingdom Building Ministries' website at www.kbm.org or call 1-800-873-8957.

THE MISSION AMERICA COALITION

The Mission America Coalition is the largest coordinated evangelistic coalition in the world. More than 350 national organizations and 210,000 churches are united for evangelism, along with hundreds of thousands of individual members. The Lighthouse Movement grew out of this coalition. A new initiative called Turn on the Light, America! is an organized effort to mobilize the church to pray for, care for, and share Christ with every man, woman, and child in America. Resources include access to the latest evangelism tools and tactics God has raised up for "such a time as this." Alongside that mission is a parallel emphasis on seeking God for the revival of His church and the spiritual transformation of our nation. For information on how you can be involved, visit www.missionamerica.org.

Notes

1. Laura Pappano, *The Connection Gap: Why Americans Feel So Alone* (New Brunswick, N. J.: Rutgers University Press, 2001), p. 8.

2. Cheryl Mendelson, *Home Comforts: The Art and Science of Keeping House* (New York: Scribner, 1999), pp. 7-8.

3. These *Neighborhood Ideas for Caring* are representative of ideas you'll find through the Mission America Coalition's emphasis on evangelism. Go to www.missionamerica.org for more information.

4. Many thanks to Alvin VanderGriend of the Lighthouse Movement, who developed this acronym.

About the Authors

Norm and Becky Wretlind are the cofounders of NeighborHope Ministries. Through their training materials and seminars, they are equipping thousands of Christians around the world to host evangelistic Christmas parties and other neighborhood gatherings. Norm and Becky have been married thirty-eight years and live in Littleton, Colorado. They have two married daughters, Miriam and Mindi, two godly "sons-in-love," and eight precious grandchildren.

Jim Killam is a freelance journalist and college journalism teacher. Since 1996, he has been a regular contributor and columnist for *Christianity Today*'s *Marriage Partnership* magazine. He and his wife, Lauren, have three children: Ben, Zack, and Lindsey. They live in Poplar Grove, Illinois.